THE NEW
INTERNATIONAL
WEBSTER'S
POCKET
COMPUTER
DICTIONARY
OF THE ENGLISH LANGUAGE

◆◆◆

This edition exclusive to

IDF
INTERNATIONAL

(949) 587-9207

Published by
Trident Press International

Cover Design Copyright © Trident Press International
Text Copyright © 1997 J. Radcliffe

ISBN 1-55280-273-6

Printed in Peru

IMPORTED BY/IMPORTE PAR
DS-MAX CANADA
RICHMOND HILL, ONTARIO
L4B 1H7

ENGLAND
WENTWALK LTD.
278A ABBEYDALE ROAD, WEMBLEY
MIDDLESEX, HA0 1NT

MALAYSIA
PRO ENTERPRISE SDN BHD
LOT 605, SS13/1K, OFF JLN.
KEWAJIPAN, 47500 SUBANG JAYA
SELANGOR D.E., MALAYSIA

DS-MAX
FOOTHILL RANCH, CA 92610-2619
IMPORTER: #16-1241510
949-587-9207

A

abend *abnormal ending*
The termination of processing due to a program or system fault.

abort
To terminate a process before completion. Generally used in reference to a mainframe program, especially one that has gone awry. In the world of PC's, we are more inclined to *exit* a program or command with the *Escape key*.

ABS *ABSolute value of n*
A programming language term used by many **spreadsheet** and **database** applications to return the **absolute value** of a number.

absolute value
The value of a number without regard to its sign; most often used in a **spreadsheet** or **database** formula when the result of a calculation that may be positive or negative needs to be converted to a positive number for additional calculation.

abstract
To briefly summarize or compile; the summary or compilation so created.

ACC
See **accumulator**, **accuracy control characters**

accelerator chip
The main driver of a video card, a chip that speeds the processing of graphics data.

access
To call up or activate for use. A computer system may contain a variety of programs and data files, but none are active or ready for use until called up by

1

access code

the operator or a program routine. In addition, the computer may require drivers or system files to access a peripheral, such as a printer or scanner.

access code

The user name or security code required to use a computer, a particular program, or certain files. Computer files protected by an access code require that the user type in his or her code before the protected files can be made available.

access time

The interval between a request for data from storage by the computer and the moment when it is available to the user.

accounting check

A routine to assure that data has been entered and processed accurately.

accumulator, accumulator register

The computer register which stores the intermediate results of arithmetical and logical operations.

accuracy control character

A special character used to signal that transmitted data is faulty or unsuited to a particular device.

acoustic coupler

A device for connecting the computer to a telephone hand set to allow transmission of computer data over the telephone lines when a more direct connection is not available

acronym

A word formed from the first letter or combination of letters of a compound name. For example, *COBOL*, a programming language, is derived from *COmmon Business Oriented Language*. See also, **BASIC**.

active document
A document that is currently available to manipulation by the user.

active file
A computer file available to the user or the computer for processing.

active matrix
A type of *LCD* computer screen display that is constantly refreshed by means of transistors embedded in the screen. Characterized by high contrast and a brilliant image, its weight and heavy power requirements make it less than ideal for portables. See also, *passive*.

active window
In a system that allows viewing of multiple documents or programs on the screen, the document or window that is currently selected and available to the user.

ACU See *automatic calling unit*

adapter
Any hardware device or software routine that makes disparate hardware or software elements compatible.

adaptive system
A computer program that "learns" by maintaining a record of its activity and revising subsequent actions. An *OCR* or *optical character recognition* program, for example, may consistently fail to correctly recognize a certain character; once corrections are fed into the program, an adaptive system will adjust its matrix to properly read the character in the future.

ADC See *analog to digital converter*

3

add–on
A hardware or software supplement that serves to enhance performance of an existing program or device.

add–on card
A removable computer circuit board used to control a peripheral device such as a parallel or serial port, a game port, a scanner, or accelerated video.

address
(1) A number used to identify a specific location in computer storage, also called an *absolute address*. When data is saved, the address of its location is recorded in the *file allocation table* so that it can be quickly found when next called up.
(2) See *relative address*.
(3) To call up data from a program or application.

addressing
A program instruction for assigning a memory location to a command or data.

addressing capacity
A reference to the memory available for running programs, accessing data, and performing other functions.

ADP See *automatic data processing*

advanced power management
A feature designed to save power in many newer computers that powers down the screen and, in some cases, the hard drive when input has been suspended for a set interval, such as ten minutes.

Advanced SCSI Programming Interface
A software standard that allows a *SCSI* controller to communicate with other software.

AI See *artificial intelligence*.

algebraic expression

A formula, such as in a spreadsheet that follows the conventions for mathematical syntax. Math lightweights, have no fear; we're not necessarily alluding to complex equations. Let's say you have the household budget listed in column A of a spreadsheet and your actual expense in column B. You want to know how much the actual varied from the budget, so you go to column C and enter the formula on row 1: B1–A1; one line 2: B2–A2; and so on. The results in column C will show how much over and under budget you are for each item, and B1–A1 is an algebraic expression.

algorithm

A set of precise instructions for performing a specific task and that must have a finite number of steps and a definite stopping place. Computer programs and routines are algorithms, but there are simpler examples: the IRS has often used algorithmic diagrams in literature designed to assist the taxpayer in determining what forms to use or qualification for certain benefits.

alias

A name assigned to a file or a block of data, used to address it for processing. When using a *lookup table* in a spreadsheet, for example, it's more practical to give the table an easily remembered name relating to its purpose than it is to spell out the location of the data each time it is referred to in a formula.

alignment

(1) The placement of type in a line, as flush right,

allocation

centered, justified, etc.

(2) The positioning of a *frame*, artwork, or a block of type in relation to its placement on a page.

allocation

The assignment of computer resources for a specific purpose, such as an area of memory set aside for the operation of a *TSR*.

alphameric Same as *alphanumeric*.

alphanumeric

Short for *alphabetical/numeric*; descriptive of a string that is may contain both letters and numbers.

Alternate key *(Alt)*

A type of control key used in conjunction with other keys to modify their actions or to execute commands.

ALU *Arithmetic and Logic Unit*

That part of the *CPU* that performs *arithmetic* and *logic* functions.

ambiguous

Imprecise; of a program command or formula stated in such a way that it may yield an undesirable or unreliable result.

American National Standards Institute

An organization concerned with standardization of computer elements.

American Standard Code for Information Exchange

A standardized code for representing print and control characters for the computer.

American Standards Association

The forerunner of the *American National Standards Institute*.

amplification
The process of increasing a signal or sound.
amplifier
A device that boosts a signal to increase its output strength.
analog
Descriptive of data represented as a continuous variable, such as sound or an electrical impulse.
analog signal
An electric signal used to transmit information, such as by a conventional telephone.
analog to digital converter
A device that converts analog signals, such as those from a telephone, to digital data that can be processed by the computer.
analysis
(1) The separation of something into its component parts so as to study it.
(2) In the world of computers, the methodical study of a program, routine, formula, etc. to explore the nature of its actions or to resolve a problem.
(3) Use of the computer to compile and examine data, such as for the finances of a business.
analyst
(1) One experienced in identifying the source of problems and suggesting the means to correct them, especially for a computer program.
(2) One who is able to direct the compilation of business data and assess it carefully to predict trends, potential problems, and opportunities.
anchor, anchor point
(1) The starting point for selection of a block of copy

for editing, printing, etc.

(2) A reference point or exact position for fixing the place of extraneous matter such as graphics or sound in a document.

AND operator

A Boolean operator used to return a value of *true* if the statements it joins are both true. The *AND operator* may be used, for example, to define a selection such as for a **spreadsheet** or **database** formula that seeks to choose from a list those entries that have certain things in common—all those who are customers *and* live in a particular city; all those who are employees *and* have over ten years of service. The syntax, or precise way in which the *AND operator* is used varies depending on the program in which it is used.

annotation

(1) An explanatory note.

(2) In a computer program or routine, an annotation may be a heading or a comment explaining the function of a command or series of commands. The annotation serves as an aid to tracking a series of actions, especially for anyone working on the program in the future, and is marked in some way so that the computer will not mistake it for a command.

(3) A feature in some programs that allows commentary or corrections to be attached to a file for later review by others without changing the original document.

ANSI See *American National Standards Institute*.

anti–virus

A program or routine designed to detect any

unauthorized or undesirable alteration of a computer or its programs.

APL *A Programming Language*

An interactive computer programming language notably proficient in operations involving arrays.

APM See *advanced power management*.

append

To add, as a supplement.

APPEND

An operating system command which enables programs to open files in designated directories as though the files were included in the current directory.

application

(1) A computer program designed for a particular use, such as a word processor or spreadsheet.

(2) A particular use to which a program is applied, as for compiling financial transactions or inventory records.

application development

The process of combining and arranging computer routines to create a program designed for a particular use. Application development programs or systems complete with standard routines are designed to simplify the process of creating applications, eliminating the need to program each new application from scratch.

application generator

A feature in some computer programs that assists the user with a program designed to create custom applications. In some cases, the application can be made a stand–alone utility that does not require the

application program

full program to run.

application program

A computer software package used to perform a variety of related tasks such as for accounting, word processing, desktop publishing, etc.

approximation

A value which is only nearly correct; a number that has been rounded or truncated.

architecture

The design of a computer that defines such things as type of processor, transfer speed, bus size, etc.

archive

(1) A file *attribute* assigned automatically by the computer system each time a computer file is saved. The *archive attribute* is often used in incremental backup routines—the program copies only those files with the archive flag set and deletes the flag after the file is backed up.

(2) A collection of files seldom if ever used, but that are saved because they may of value at some future date.

area

A segment of computer storage set aside for a particular purpose and that cannot be moved or used for any other purpose, such as for virtual memory.

argument

A value or variable in a formula, as in *2+4*, wherein + is the *operator*, and both *2* and *4* are *arguments*.

arithmetic

Concerning or involved with mathematics; the addition, subtraction, multiplication, and division of numbers.

arithmetic and logic unit See *ALU*.

arithmetic expression

A formula that uses a mathematical operator and returns a numeric value.

arithmetic processor See *math coprocessor*.

arithmetic relation

An expression that uses a mathematical operator to show the relationship between two values, such as = (equal to), ≠ (not equal to), < (lesser than), or > (greater than).

arrangement

The way in which items are located or displayed in a set or array.

array

An ordered group of like elements: a *one dimensional array* may be a list of numbers representing total expense for each department in a company; to show expense by type, a *two dimensional array* is necessary, with a column for each department and rows for each type of expense; a *three dimensional array* may be prepared with layers to represent similar data for other periods.

art

Any computer element that is not text. See *graphics*, *object*, *picture*.

artificial cognition See *OCR*.

artificial intelligence

Descriptive of the ability of a computer to simulate human intelligence, as by recording corrections to its output and adjusting for future transactions. See also, *adaptive system*.

artificial language
A computer programming language with a distinct set of rules and vocabulary.

art program See *draw program*.

ASA *American Standards Association*
The forerunner of the **American National Standards Institute**.

ASAD
Association of Shareware Authors and Distributors

ascending sort
An alphabetical or numerical arrangement that progresses from lowest to highest.

ASCII See **American Standard Code for Information Exchange**.

ASCII file
A text document that contains only the printed and control characters as defined by the ASCII standard and none of the more sophisticated formatting such as for special fonts, styles, tabs, etc. provided by most word processing or desktop publishing programs. Despite the efforts of software vendors to achieve at least limited compatibility with others, not all text files can be read by other programs. ASCII bridges that gap—a file saved in ASCII format from one program can be read by another (sans special formatting, of course), or even exchanged across *platforms*.

ASK
A programmed query, requesting input from the user; often used for directing a batch file or inputting information to a database. When the *ASK* command is executed, the program is paused to wait for

input from the user.

aspect ratio

The relationship or proportion of the horizontal to the vertical measurement as of a computer monitor screen or of a graphics element.

ASPI See *Advanced SCSI Programming Interface*.

assemble

To translate or convert computer program instructions from an *artificial language* or *programming language* into *machine language* that can be understood directly by the computer.

assembler

A type of program that translates a *programming language* into simple instructions that are understood directly by the computer.

It's time someone told you the truth—the computer is stupid! *Really* stupid! It operates basically with millions of microscopic *flip-flops* (think of them as switches) that can be set to either of two states (such as open or closed—computer programmers refer to them as 0 or 1). Each command to the computer requires passage through sets of flip-flops arrayed in a variety of ways to recognize and execute the command.

Consider what an action as simple as striking a letter on the keyboard requires:

> that the CPU be alerted that something has happened,
> that it record what happened,
> that it determine what it means,
> that it look up instructions for output (print to screen or directly to a printer for example),

> that it form and display it on screen, etc.
—all conveyed through yes/no, true/false, or 0/1 instructions.

Consider, too, that early programmers had to set up instructions to the computer in this 0/1 language and refine or debug those programs by sifting through reams of printed 0/1 data.

As programs increased in complexity you can imagine how unwieldy all of this became. Gradually, ever more sophisticated systems were developed; systems that permitted programming in something approximating "normal" language and arithmetic notation. While still somewhat arcane, these computer programming languages nevertheless ease somewhat the difficulty in developing complex programs. But, alas, the computer can't learn those new language and so a translator, the *assembler* or **compiler**, is necessary to produce a translation after the program is written and before it can be executed.

assignment statement

A command that assigns the value of an expression to a variable name, as $A=A+1$, in which the value of A increases by one for each iteration of the command. Such a command may be used in a routine to step through the records in a database—once the routine (such as a search for records in a particular zip code) has been executed for one record, the assignment statement is invoked to reset the variable (in this case a record number); the variable is then increased by one and the routine is again executed.

asynchronous communication

The recognition and transmission of data as it

becomes available rather than at timed intervals. Asynchronous communication is more or less continuous because data is transmitted as it becomes available without the constraints of a timing device.

asynchronous data transmission

Same as *asynchronous communication.*

attenuation

The reduction of a signal's strength without distortion as it passes through a computer system.

attribute

A distinct characteristic, as of a program variable or a computer file. See also *file attribute*.

audio

(1) Relating to sound frequencies within the range of the human ear.

(2) The reproduction of sound.

(3) The sound portion of a multimedia presentation or program.

audio system

(1) A computer capable of responding to voice commands.

(2) The sound card, speakers, software, etc. that combine to produce sound from the computer.

audio–visual

The integration of sound and sight to present information in a program.

audit program, audit software

A computer program designed to validate data.

audit trail

(1) The tracking of a computer program through each command to verify the actions taken.

(2) A means for confirming the validity of the

augment

transactions in an accounting system.

augment

To expand or supplement the function or capabilities of, as by the addition of software or hardware to increase the processing speed or memory in a computer.

auto dial

(1) The dialing of a telephone link automatically at a pre-determined time, as for an automatic backup or the downloading of data to a remote location.

(2) The ability of a computer program to dial a telephone on command, as from a personal phone directory in the computer.

auto–index

A feature in some word processing and desktop publishing programs which creates an index from the text.

auto loader

(1) The ROM program that initializes the operating system when a computer is brought on line.

(2) A program which directs that a program be loaded automatically based on some contingency. The program may be activated by a timer, such as for downloading data or processing records during the night hours; by equipment failure, wherein the called program reroutes data or calls a supervisor; or by a signal from a remote location in order to provide access from the remote station.

automatic

A reference to processes and devices that operate without further human involvement once the procedure has been established.

automatic backup

(1) A program feature that creates a backup copy of a file each time changes are saved.

(2) A program or routine that backs up data in the computer at a predetermined time, usually set to operated at the end of the day or during other off hours.

automatic calling unit, automatic dialing unit

A device programmed to dial telephone numbers in a prearranged sequence.

automatic data processing

The manipulation of data with the use of a computer.

automatic link

A connection between an *object* inserted from another application that provides for the update of all instances of the object when a change is made in the original. For example, a *table* from a *spreadsheet* showing sales by territory may be included in a memo to all sales personnel. If there is a *link* between the files, the table in the memo can be updated on command whenever changes are made to the spreadsheet. An *automatic link* provides for updating whenever the memo file is opened.

automatic load

To bring a program in computer memory on line by a predetermined signal, as of a timer. An *automatic load* may be used to create backup files or to transfer files to a remote location during normal down time. See also, *auto loader*.

automatic routine

See *auto loader*, *automatic load*.

available resources
(1) All of the processing capacity, memory, storage, and peripherals available to a computer system.
(2) Those resources which remain ready and available for use after discounting those occupied by primary processing, such as the RAM space remaining after a program is loaded.

.AVI *Audio Video Interleaved*
The file extension for a video file with a sound track.

axis (*pl.* **axes**)
A straight reference line on a graph that may be horizontal, vertical, or on a plane that is perpendicular to both the horizontal and vertical lines.

B

Babbage, Charles
Inventor of the analytical engine, forerunner of the computer.

background noise
Extraneous matter such as random dots in a scanned image or static in electronic transmission.

background processing
Computer operations that take place out of view, such as printing from a buffer or compiling of a database, while the user has control of the computer and is able to manipulate other data or files in the foreground.

backlit supertwist LCD
A computer display screen used mainly for portable microcomputers which uses LCD technology coupled with the addition of a backlighted panel for a brighter screen and improved contrast

back slash

A computer keyboard symbol (\ ) used in some operating systems to separate directory and file names. For example in DOS, "C:\BIN\HIMEM.SYS" means that the file HIMEM.SYS is located in the BIN directory on the C drive.

back up

To make a copy of data for safe keeping.

One of the most important, and least followed, maxims for the computer operator is to regularly back up data. A computer **crash** that damages the read/write head will in all likelihood damage the disk as well, eliminating all hope of recovering the data contained on the disk. Backup copies of program disks and a recent backup of data files stored on a removable disk or tape insure that once a damaged computer is repaired or replaced, the operator can be up and running in a matter of hours with a minimum loss of data.

Program and computer configuration files that are changed from time to time should also be backed up periodically to insure that user–defined configuration is restored when operation is resumed—they are easy to find: simply scout the boot and program directories for files that are dated more recently than the bulk of the program files.

backup copy

A copy of program and data files on a removable medium such as a floppy disk or tape, kept as protection against corruption of the original files. Keep in mind that most media degrades over time so that even though frequent recopying of programs and unchanged data isn't necessary, it's probably wise to back up the entire computer at least once a year.

backup system

(1) Computer hardware available to take over processing in the event of a failure of the primary computer system, most common in large–scale systems such as mainframes and networks.

(2) The means for recovering from a primary system failure. The system may be simply a written procedure for reloading programs and data or it may be a program that handles the task. There are software packages that back up the entire disk, then permit incremental backups of configuration and data files (much faster than a full disk backup); to recover from a disk failure, the full backup is restored, then the incremental backup is added for those files that are new or newer.

backward compatibility

The ability of a program upgrade to use files created with an earlier version of the program.

banner

A headline, usually a name or title, that stretches across the top of a document such as a newsletter or press release.

bar chart

A diagram that translates quantities into columns of varying length according to their relative magnitude. Most newer spreadsheet programs have the ability to create the chart from spreadsheet data with a minimum input from the user.

bar code

A pattern of thick and thin lines and spaces that

represent characters that can be read by a **scanner**. The *bar code* identifies the item to which it is affixed; the scanner transfers the signal to a computer that matches the code to a price, inventory unit, etc.

barrel distortion
Condition of a computer screen image that is narrowed at the top and bottom, and bowed outward in the center.

base, base number
The value on which a numbering system is founded, for example, the binary system on base 2, the octal system on base 8, the decimal system on base 10, and the hexadecimal system on base 16.

baseline
The imaginary line on which a row of type rests and ⌄ by which position is determined. For example, *superscript* or *subscript* may be specified to be positioned a certain number of *points* above or below the baseline respectively.

BASIC *Beginner's All-purpose Symbolic Instruction Code*
A relatively simple programming language.

basic code
Computer instructions written in **machine language**. Not to be confused with *BASIC code,* instructions written in BASIC programming language.

Basic Input/Output System *BIOS*
The part of the operating system that controls communication with a monitor screen, keyboard, printer, and other peripheral devices.

.BAT
The *file name extension* for a *batch file*.

batch
A group of files or commands that are processed as a unit.

batch command
A single instruction that causes the execution of a number of relatively simple commands contained in a *batch file*. A batch file is a program file so that the name of the file is the command that causes the operating system to execute commands within the file.

batch file
A program file containing a series of commands that are processed in order. Batch files are somewhat easy to write and are often employed by users who are not programmers to simplify the operation of their machines. For example, the user may prefer not facing a blank screen when the computer boots up—a batch file can be created to display a menu of the applications available with a reminder of the command line for accessing each program. A batch file can be made more sophisticated, with an interface that allows selection of a program by entering a single letter or number and an instruction to return to the menu when the program is closed.

battery backup See *uninterruptible power supply*.

baud, baud rate
A measure of transmission speed, equivalent to about 1 bit per second.

bay
A space in a computer cabinet where a hardware device such as a floppy disk, CD, or tape drive can be or has been installed.

BBS See *Bulletin Board Service*

benchmark
A standard by which computers, computer chips, programs, peripherals, etc. can be measured or compared.

benchmark program
A program designed to test a particular device, such as the speed at which a particular computer chip or program processes data.

Bernoulli Box
A type of removable hard disk and drive.

beta testing
The use of a new or extensively revised computer program by a group of select users in order to unearth any bugs that need to be corrected before the program is released on the open market.

bi–directional
Descriptive of a device that functions in two directions such as a bi–directional bus that can carry signals both to and from the devices to which it is connected or a bi–directional printer that prints as it passes over the paper in either direction.

binary code, binary coded character
The representation of characters by the use of binary numbers.

binary digit
The digits in a binary system, *0* or *1*.

binary logic
Reasoning in computer formulae that returns one of two possible variables, as *true* or *false, yes* or *no*.

binary search
A technique for searching through sequenced data

binary system

by dividing the set in half, discarding the half that logically does not contain the search object, dividing the remaining set in half, and so on until the search object is found.

binary system

A number system in base 2.

bionics *BIo electrONICS*

The use of biological principles in the design of electronic systems.

BIOS See *Basic Input/Output System*.

bit *Binary digIT*

The basic unit in the binary system.

bitmap

A type of computer graphic image made up of tiny dots (pixels), each of which is assigned a series of bits to record its precise location.

bitmap font

A typeface of a specific size and style whose characters are made up of pixel patterns and that are available through hardware (see *font cartridge*) or a software program.

See also, *scalable font*, *software font*.

blank

In a computer file, the absence of data; not a space or zero.

bleed

Designed to print off the edge of a page, as a picture or graphic.

block

(1) A collection of data, files, etc. that is or can be manipulated as a unit.

(2) A fixed–size data string transmitted as a unit.

(3) A selection of adjoining data, as in a word processor or spreadsheet, to be copied, moved, formatted, etc. as a unit.

block command

An instruction that acts on all elements in a block of text or files.

block sort

A technique for sorting data or database records that entails splitting the records into small groups, sorting them, then reintegrating the groups.

.BMP *Bitmap*

A file name extension for a bitmapped image, a type of graphics file.

bold, boldface

Descriptive of type designed with thick, heavy lines. The terms at the beginning of this entry are set in boldface.

bomb

A situation wherein the computer ceases to process or respond to commands from the keyboard, mouse, etc. and must be restarted, often with an accompanying loss of data. A *crash*.

Yes, a computer can become confused! In the course of transferring 50,000 to 100,000 bits of data or more *per second* it is inevitable that an errant signal will creep in now and then. Mostly, the computer is able to correct such problems on its own, but occasionally it can't and the result is a lost chain or a corrupted file. Good work habits that include saving one's work should preclude the possibility of losing very much data. If the computer bombs or crashes again shortly after the reboot, it's wise to run a

bookmark

utility program such as CHKDSK or SCANDISK in DOS to find and eliminate any corrupted files or chains

bookmark

A user–specified reference marker in a computer file that allows instant selection from another location. Bookmarks can be used to access various sections of a document or spreadsheet to facilitate editing.

Boolean algebra

A system of calculation based on Boolean logic.

Boolean logic

A logic system based on a return of one of two variables, as *true* or *false*, *yes* or *no*. Boolean logic utilizes operators such as *AND*, *OR*, *NOT*, *IF*, and *THEN*.

boot

To initialize a computer by powering it up and loading its operating system.

bootleg software

A program obtained outside of normal channels, such as proprietary software transferred illegally to a second user.

bootstrap

A disc, device, or routine that loads the operating system into a computer enabling it to function.

bps *bits per second*

A measure of data transmission speed

branch

A command to jump to another section of a program: an *unconditional branch* directs a move to a specific location; a *conditional branch* first calls for a test, then directs a move when certain conditions are met.

brightness
Descriptive of the reflective quality of a medium holding copy to be scanned.

Break (key)
A command key that temporarily suspends processing.

brownout
A reduction in the line voltage to a computer that can cause loss of data and damage to computer hardware over time.

browse
(1) The process of scanning the contents of a file.
(2) A database program feature for scanning records in which the fields are aligned in columns much like a spreadsheet. This technique permits the user to sort and then rapidly scan the selected fields in search of desired information.

bubble sort
An algorithm for sorting text, database records, etc. in which the first two elements of the set are put in order, then the second and third are compared and ordered, and so on through the entire set. This creates a partial sort and by default pushes the highest item to the end of the list. The process is then repeated from the beginning until the entire list is in order.

buffer
An area for temporary storage of data, often used to free resources or to compensate for a difference in transmission speeds between devices.

bug
A defect in a computer system or program.

bug patch
An instruction or routine added to a program to cir-
cumvent a bug. Bugs are not uncommon in new
programs or extensive upgrades of old ones. Nor is it
uncommon for the vendor to offer a free 'fix' or patch
to correct the problem. Not all bugs are the fault of
the programmer, however; many are caused by
changes in technology that hit the market after the
program was introduced. And most software vendors
jump on them quickly to offer a fix for those as well.

bullet
A heavy dot or other symbol used at the beginning of
a line to set it off; usually one of a series of such
lines.

Bulletin Board Service
A message center that is accessed by computer users via telephone data lines for the exchange of information, computer files, etc.

bundled
Descriptive of computer hardware and software sold
together as a package.

burn–in
(1) A method of testing for weak components in a
computer.
(2) A latent image on a computer monitor screen that
appears over time and is caused by leaving the same
image on the screen for long periods. Burn–in is
most common in machines that are used all day
every day with a frame or overlay that never
changes. Improved technology in the manufacture of
screens and *screen savers* have largely eliminated
the problem.

bus

(1) The set of lines which carries signals between the CPU and computer peripherals such as video graphics board, disk controller, modem, scanner, or printer.

(2) A type of computer network that provides for the placing of terminals along a straight line.

bus controller

The regulating mechanism that handles the flow of data through a computer. ·

business application

A program designed for business use, such as for payroll or inventory control.

bus mastering

A controller routine that transfers data directly to system memory from a hard disk, bypassing the CPU.

byte

(1) A basic unit of data manipulated by the computer, usually eight bits.

(2) The space required to store a single printed character.

(3) A computer word.

C

C

A structured programming language.

cable

The transmission link between devices in a computer system.

cable connector

Any of a variety of terminals or plugs used to join

cables or to connect various parts of the computer or peripherals.

cache, cache memory
A fast memory **buffer** for holding frequently called data.

cache memory hit ratio
A comparison between the total number of calls for data and the number of times that data was found in a cache. Used to measure the effectiveness of a cache.

CAD/CAM *Computer Aided Design/Computer Aided Manufacturing*
A computer program used to aid in the design of a product and to plan for its manufacture.

CADD *Computer Aided Design and Drafting*
A graphics program that assists in the creation of engineering drawings.

CAE *Computer Aided Engineering*
A program or programs that use the computer to assess the design of structures, systems, etc.

CAI *Computer Aided Instruction*
(1) The use of computers and computer programs in teaching.
(2) The use of computers and computer programs for the administrative tasks associated with teaching, such as for preparing lessons, tracking attendance and grades, etc.

CAL *Computer Augmented Learning*
The reinforcement of learning with the use of the computer.

calculator
Any device designed to perform mathematical

computations.

calendar date

A date expressed as the month, day, and year as contrasted to a *Julian date*.

camera–ready copy

A computer printout that is ready for reproduction by a commercial printer.

cancel

A command to a computer to reverse a change made in an application or to stop a procedure, as a *database sort*.

canned software

Computer programs that are available to a wide range of users. The popularity and success of today's personal computer can be attributed in part to the large variety of reasonably priced programs that are available to the user.

capacity

(1) The physical size of a storage device.

(2) The ability of a computer or peripheral to manage a particular task or series of tasks.

card See *add–on card*.

card edge connector

A slotted plug which links an add–on card to a computer.

card slot

A channel inside a computer case with a connection for installing a printed circuit board for an *add–on* device.

carriage

The device on an impact printer that holds the paper.

carriage return

A term that remains in computer jargon as a vestige of the old manual typewriter with a moveable carriage and a fixed printing head. Comparable in some ways to the *Enter key* on a computer keyboard, the *word wrap* feature in most word processing programs has made the term outmoded except when working with an *ASCII file* and in printer programming. Because of the word wrap feature, the Enter key is usually used to signal the end of a paragraph instead of the end of a line. An ASCII file, however, does not include word wrap so that, as in printer programming, the end of each line must be marked.

Cartesian coordinate

One of the set of numbers that locates a point in space on a two– or three–dimensional Cartesian coordinate system. *Cartesian coordinates* are used by drawing or drafting programs to represent lines and forms.

Cartesian coordinate system

A means for locating a point on a plane (a two-dimensional system) or a solid (a three–dimensional system) by a number that represents the distance from a point where two or three perpendicular lines intersect.

cartridge

A container, as for a magnetic tape.

case

An attribute of type, as *uppercase* (capitalized) or *lowercase*, so called for the shallow case in which hand set type was stored.

case conversion
   (1) The changing of the attribute of text, as from capitals to lower case.
   (2) A word processing program feature that uses a command or hot key to change the case of type.
case sensitive
   Descriptive of a command or search instruction that must follow exactly the type format, as capital or lower case, in order to obtain correct results.
catenate
   To connect in a series; create a *character string*.
cathode-ray tube See *CRT*.
CD See *compact disk*.
CDPD *Cellular Digital Packet Data*
   A collection of data transmitted as a unit over cellular telephone lines.
CD ROM *Compact Disk Read-Only Memory*
   A compact disk containing data that can be read but that cannot be altered. The large amount of space available on a CD makes it ideal for storing video images and sound.
cell
   (1) An area in computer memory that holds a unit of information, such as a character.
   (2) A basic unit of data in a spreadsheet.
.CFG
   File name extension for a *configuration* file.
CGA *Color Graphics Adaptor*
   An early standard for the display of graphics on a computer color monitor screen.
.CGM *Computer Graphics Metafile*
   A file name extension for a vector image, a type of

character

graphics file.

character

Any of the set of letters, numbers, and symbols used to represent information.

character code

A set of binary digits that represents a specific letter, number, or symbol.

character pitch See *pitch*.

character printer

(1) A printer with output limited to a fixed font in the manner of a typewriter, such as a *daisy-wheel* printer.

(2) A printer that cannot print graphics, or that can print only the graphic symbols in an *extended character set*.

character reader

A device used to scan and record characters or symbols that are converted into digital data.

character recognition

The identification of text or special symbols by any of a variety of input devices.

character set

(1) All of the characters or symbols used or recognized by a particular device or system.

(2) All of the characters contained in a particular font of type.

character string

A set of characters processed as a unit.

chart

(1) A graphic representation that depicts relationships among a group of associated values.

(2) A diagram that outlines the steps in a system or

procedure.

chassis

The framework which contains the components of a
computer or to which they are attached.

chip

A semiconductor in which an integrated circuit is
formed.

CHS *Cylinder, Head, and Sector*

A technique for addressing data on a **hard disk** by
specifying its **cylinder** location, which **read/write
head** can access the **track** where the data is located, and the position of the **sector** of the track
that actually contains the data. See also, **LBA**.

circuit

A complete path for the flow of electrical current.

circuit board

An insulated card that holds circuits, electronic
components, and connectors that comprise or drive
other computer components such as a communication port, video, a scanner, etc.

CIS *Card Information Structure*

Information on a **PCMCIA card** that outlines the
formatting and organization of data on the card.

click

To quickly press and release the button on a computer mouse or similar device to place the cursor at
a particular position on a document or to make a selection.

client

In a computer network, any workstation that can
use the resources of another, called a **server**.

clip art, clip art file
Artwork saved as a digital computer file that can be used to embellish documents, reports, etc. The name derives from an earlier, computerless environment when advertisers were furnished with sheets of artwork that could be 'clipped' for use in display ads— the practice continues, but now it is often with the aid of a computer.

clock
A device in the computer that generates recurrent pulses for keeping time and synchronizing communications.

clock–doubled
Descriptive of a computer chip that can perform certain tasks (usually internal processing) at twice its rated speed.

clone
A computer or peripheral designed to be compatible with a similar device that is accepted as a standard in the industry. Cloned devices tend to be reliable and less expensive than the standard from which they are derived, but the level of compatibility may vary.

closed loop
(1) A programming or formula routine error in which output modifies input, so that a final value is never reached, such as a spreadsheet formula in cell B that calls for the value of $A+B$ that cannot be attained, as B changes each time the command is executed. Also called an *endless loop*.
It is not uncommon, especially among inexperienced users, to inadvertently include the current cell in a

list of cells whose values are to be totaled, for example. Most programs warn of such action or prevent it.

(2) A programming technique that causes a reiteration of an instruction until a specific condition is met such as a database search that calls for stepping through each record and checking it until the end of the file is reached.

cluster

A set of *sectors* that represents the minimum file size that can be created within a *hard disk* or hard disk *partition.* A *sector* is the smallest unit of memory identified by the computer's operating system. When data is updated and saved, the computer rewrites the entire sector of 512 bytes, not merely the changes within the sector. A *cluster* is the smallest unit that can be saved as a file. The restriction is imposed by DOS's File Allocation Table (FAT) system used to identify and locate files on a disk that is limited by the number of units it can record and manage. To stay within the limit, total storage in each disk partition is divided into groups of sectors called *clusters* that vary in size according to the disk or partition size.

Back in the olden days (a couple of decades ago), a 32MB disk was the largest that the operating system would recognize, programs were simpler, and management of the countless files contained in many of today's programs was not even envisioned. As larger disks became available, they were managed by dividing them into *partitions* of 32MB or less. Ultimately, larger programs and data files called for larger partitions, and a means to work around the FAT limitation became necessary. Increasing cluster *size* of larger disks or partitions was the solution, so that a 256MB disk or partition is addressed in 4KB clusters made up of 8 sectors, a 512MB disk in 8KB clusters of 16 sectors, and so on.

A listing of computer files will show many small ones, but the minimum disk space occupied by the file is the cluster size for that disk. Unused space in the cluster cannot be used by another file, however small. A file that is even slightly larger than a cluster will occupy two clusters. The wasted space is often referred to as *file slack*, *slack space* or *cluster overhang*.

CMOS *Complimentary Metal Oxide Semiconductor*

coaxial cable

A cable made up of an outer metal tubular conductor surrounding an insulated inner conducting core, used for high-frequency transmission such as for telephone or television.

COBOL *COmmon Business Oriented Language*

A structured computer programming language for business applications that uses a vocabulary of familiar English words and phrases.

code

(1) A combination of words, characters, and symbols recognized by the computer as instructions.

(2) The process of translating instructions to computer language.

code set

A complete collection of words, characters, and symbols which are recognized as instructions in a particular computer programming language.

cold boot

Restarting a computer that is completely shut down. See also, *warm boot*.

color convergence See *convergence*.

color matching

Adjustments to the intensity of the red, green, and blue electron beams in a color monitor **CRT** to match the color displayed by a standard document. See also *convergence*.

column

The vertical arrangement of data in a two or three dimensional array.

COM

(1) *Computer Output Microfilm* Microfilm or microfiche created with the aid of a computer.

(2) *COMmunications*, as in *COM port*.

.COM

The file name extension for a command file, a program file that is activated when the file name is brought to the command line by the user or another program.

command

(1) A key word or action directing the performance of a function.

(2) An instruction to a computer.

command character

A character that expresses a control function.

command–driven

(1) Descriptive of an interactive computer program that acts on each user command as it is issued.

(2) Descriptive of a program that responds only to

command line

instructions issued from the keyboard in contrast to one that is **menu-driven**.

command line

The position at which instructions are entered by the user or a program to direct computer processing.

comment See **annotation**.

communication

The transfer of data, as between a computer and peripherals, or between two computers over telephone lines or by radio transmission.

communication buffer

A device that provides temporary storage of data that is being sent or received to allow for difference in the speed or availability of various devices.

communication link

Hardware or software that permits the transfer of data between devices.

communication protocol

Standards for the transfer of data between devices.

communication software

A program that enables the transfer of data between modems.

compact disk

A **digital** disk from which data is read by a special **laser**. The laser reads binary data as *0*'s and *1*'s by distinguishing between microscopic flat and pitted dots on the surface of the disk.

compaction See **defrag**.

COMPARE

An operating system command that contrasts files, documents, etc. for ordering or verification.

compatibility
Descriptive of the ability of hardware and software to function in harmony.

compiler
A program that translates a high–level computer programming language into machine language.

component
Any of the main elements in a computer system.

COM port *COMmunications port*
Any of the connections on a computer that permit the transfer of data as to a peripheral device or to another computer.

composition
(1) The setting of type for reproduction.
(2) The overall layout of type and graphic elements on a page. Also called *page makeup*.

compression
The technique of compacting data for more efficient storage or transmission.

compression utility
A program that compresses files for storage to save space and restores them as required for use.

computer
(1) Any device capable of performing mathematical or logical operations.
(2) A programmable machine that stores and retrieves data, and performs high–speed logical and mathematical operations.

computer animation
(1) The creation of moving images especially of cartoons or special effects with the aid of a computer, as for television or motion pictures.

computer architecture

(2) Moving images that are controlled by or viewed with the aid of a computer.

computer architecture See *architecture*.

computer art
Artwork created with the aid of a computer.

computer game
A computer program designed for amusement or instruction.

computer graphics
Charts, graphs, diagrams, or pictures produced with the aid of the computer.

computer imaging
(1) See *computer graphics*.
(2) The enhancement or changing of photographic or drawn images with the aid of a computer.

computerize
To adapt to use or control by a computer.

computer language
A defined set of characters and symbols that are understood directly by the computer.

computer literate
Having a working knowledge of the way in which a computer operates and of at least some of the most popular software programs.

computer network See *network*.

computer run
Processing of data according to a set of programmed instructions or the output of such processing, usually associated with a business application such as for processing and writing checks for a payroll, merging updated records for a database, etc., often performed by a network server or mainframe.

computer science
The study and development of computer systems, hardware, and software.

computer security
The process of protecting a computer, computer network, or computer programs and data from access by unauthorized persons.

computer service organization
A company that provides computer related assistance to its customers such as through leasing computer time, designing and developing customized hardware and software, or maintaining a client's computer network.

computer storage See *storage*.

computer system
All of the hardware and software that can interact with a particular computer.

computer virus See *virus*.

computer word
A fixed-length set of bits comprising the smallest unit of memory that can be addressed or called up by a computer.

concatenate
To link two or more character strings.

concentrator
In a local computer network, the common connecting point for terminals in a *star* configuration. Also called a *hub*.

concurrent processing See *multitasking*.

conditional branch
A computer instruction that is executed only if certain specific conditions are met.

configuration
(1) The way in which a computer and peripherals in a system are connected and programmed to function together.
(2) The basic attributes of an application or device, often under control of the user, such as specifying how an application appears on screen or the direction of output to a certain type of printer.

connect time
The amount of time that a user is on line with a remote service or station.

console
(1) The portion of a computer that houses the device used to communicate with the CPU, such as a control panel or keyboard.
(2) A remote station on a network often consisting of only a keyboard and monitor screen.

constant
A symbol or name that represents a fixed value.

context sensitive help
The ability of some programs to pop up a help screen with information about a menu feature that is highlighted or as an adjunct to a dialogue box.

continuous-tone
Of a graphic image in which areas of color or light and shadow gradually blend, such as in a photograph. In a computer image, as in printing, the eye is fooled into perceiving the same blending when the image is reproduced with dots of varying size and density.

contrast
The relative difference in the reflection of light

between image and non–image areas in copy to be scanned.

control character
A non–printing ASCII character that is used to issue a command to a computer.

control key
Any of several keyboard keys that have a special purpose such as *Control, Home, Page Up, Shift,* or *Escape.*

Control key *Ctrl*
A control key that is used in conjunction with other keys to modify their actions or to execute commands.

controller
The interface that connects devices and the *CPU* in a computer. See also, *bus mastering, IRQ.*

convergence
Alignment of the electron beams in a *CRT* used to produce a color image. The CRT used by most monitors to create a color image does so by firing electron beams that activate *phosphors* on the surface of the screen to flash as red, green, or blue. Misalignment of beams for the respective colors degrades color reproduction, and an "out of register" appearance or halo effect, especially near the edges of the screen.

conversational language
Computer programming language commands that approximate spoken language.

conversion
The changing of a computer data file format to adapt it for a different use, as from a word processing

converter

document to a spreadsheet, or to make it compatible with a different program.

converter

(1) Software for changing data so as to use it in a different format or program.

(2) A hardware connector that permits linking of devices that would otherwise be incompatible or unable to communicate.

coordinate system

The use of symbols to locate an element or point in a two or three dimensional array.

coprocessor

An auxiliary chip that augments the functions of the *CPU*.

copy

(1) To make a duplicate, as of a file or group of files.

(2) To make a duplicate of text or graphics for insertion elsewhere in a document.

(3) *Hard copy*.

copy and paste

The process of duplicating text or graphics and placing the copied material in another position in the document, spreadsheet, etc.

cordless mouse

A computer mouse that is not wired directly to a computer, but that communicates with a receiver attached to the computer.

corona wire

The wire in an electrostatic printer that attracts toner to the surface of the paper.

cpi

Characters per inch; descriptive of a type font.

cps
Characters per second; a measure of the speed of an impact printer.

CPU *Central Processing Unit*
The integrated circuits that control the operation of a microcomputer.

CR See *carriage return.*

crash
(1) A computer or program failure.
(2) A disk failure caused by the read/write head striking the disk.

crop
In desktop publishing, trimming off unwanted parts of a picture, drawing, or other graphic image.

CRT *Cathode-Ray Tube*
A type of picture tube used as a computer monitor screen. The image is created by firing beams of electrons at **phosphors** that coat the inside of the tube; the phosphors, when struck, emit a burst of light. With a **refresh rate** of 60 times per second or greater, the burst appears to be a steady image

cryptograph
A system for encoding data files in the computer to prevent access by unauthorized users.

Ctrl See *Control Key.*

cursor
The dash, block, or other symbol on a monitor screen that marks the insertion point for text or graphics, or the location where the next action is to take place.

cursor arrows
Arrows on the keyboard that serve to move the

cursor control key

insertion point up, down, right, or left.

cursor control key
Any of the various keys that move the insertion point without altering the screen image, as arrow keys, Tab, End, Home, Page Up, or Page Down.

cut and paste
The process of deleting text or graphics and placing the deleted material in another position in the document, spreadsheet, etc.

cyberspace
(1) *Virtual reality*.
(2) The domain of those linked by computer via international networks, bulletin board services, etc.

cylinder
All of the tracks that occupy a specific position one above the other in a stack of computer storage disks that make up a *hard disk*.

D

daisy-chain bus
A *bus* system which allows peripherals to be connected in series.

daisy wheel
A type of impact printer in which the printed image is created by raised characters mounted on a rotating wheel.

.DAT
File name extension for a *configuration* file.

data (*sing.* **datum**)
Information, as that processed by a computer.

data bank
A stockpile of information available to a computer

such as that contained in a database.

database

(1) An application used to store and manipulate data. The application may be a simple one that provides for *flat files* only and that cannot be programmed, or it may have the capability of producing databases that are *programmable* and *relational*.

(2) A collection of specific related information.

database field

The part of a database *record* that contains a specific item of information; the basic unit of a database record.

database file

A file made up of records of information in distinct, related fields.

database set

A group of linked database files containing related data. For example, a *set* may contain one database with customer names and addresses, another database with price and quantity information about items held in inventory for sale, and a third database with a record of orders entered. Creating an invoice or statement may involve combining the customer information (complete with mailing address and terms) and the order information which is supplemented by pricing from the inventory database.

database sort

The arranging of records in a database according to a user–specified criteria.

data block

A selection of data records based on a specific search criterion.

data collection
(1) The process of accumulating data from hard copy or from automatically recording transactions such as at a cash register.
(2) The process of gathering data from remote locations for processing.

data collection system
The collection of hardware and software necessary for accumulating data from remote terminals.

data conversion
An altering of selected data for transfer to a different program or format, as from a database file to a spreadsheet file.

data entry
The entering or updating of information in a computer file.

data field
Any of the areas in a database dedicated to a particular item of information, as a date or a name.

data file See *database file, file*.

data format
(1) The configuration of a block of information or of a computer file, such as for text, spreadsheet, etc.
(2) The type of information acceptable in a particular field of a database record, such as a date, a number, an alphameric, etc.

data link
(1) A connection between computer systems that allows information sharing.
(2) A validation formula in a spreadsheet or database that limits entry of data into a cell or field based on a previous entry. (3) A link between documents

containing like information that automatically updates all documents when one is changed.

data management

The process of recording and manipulating data in the conduct of a business.

data parsing

Breaking a data string down to its basic elements for conversion to another file format, as from database fields to spreadsheet cells.

data processing

The manipulation of information, as by sorting, reformatting, or creating a report.

data record

The set of fields that comprise a unique entry in a database file.

data set

A block of related database records or files.

data structure

The way in which database records are organized.

data transmission

The transfer of information through a computer system or between remote systems.

data type

Information in a database record field that is classified according to specific characteristics:

- *Character* that can be letters, numbers, or symbols. Data in a character field can be sorted alphabetically or numerically, or identified for selection, such as all records containing the LASTNAME "Brown". Numbers in a character field are treated as text, that is, they cannot be acted on arithmetically, so that if the ZIPCODE field is designated as characters, we can select all records with a zip code of "32301", but we can't add the zip codes. (But then, who would want to?) Note that the zip codes (and certain other numbers) should not be designated as numeric as most programs will drop leading zeroes.

- *Numeric* designates a number that can be manipulated with a mathematical operator. Entry errors to a numeric field may be limited by not allowing the entry of letters or symbols in a numeric field, or by restricting entry to a range of values.

- *Date* fields can be limited to a specified format and validated, such as by checking for a date format, by checking for a legitimate date (2/29 only works in a leap year), or by restricting entry to a range of dates. Unlike numbers in text form, a range of dates can be selected and they can be used in calculations (see *date number*, below).

data validation

A means for verifying that information entered in a field of a database record is of the correct type or magnitude. Validation may also require that certain fields cannot be left blank.

date number

The numeric value for a specific date, as (1) the number of the day, month and year that represents a particular date, or (2) a number that represents the number of days from a base date, a common means of calculating intervals. Method (2) provides the means for calculation, such as for a dated accounts receivable report.

DCA *Document Content Architecture*
A word processing file format.
DDE See *Dynamic Data Exchange*.
dead file
A data file that is no longer active.
debug
To find and correct errors in a computer program or the operation of a piece of equipment.
decimal number
A value represented in base 10.
dedicated
Set aside for a specific purpose, such as an area in computer memory that is reserved for certain utilities or a transmission line reserved for network communication.
dedicated network
A computer network in which one or more computers are set aside (or *dedicated*) as **servers**; that is, used only to support **client** terminals.
default
A failure to act or issue specific instructions for the operation of a device or program.
default configuration
Instructions or formatting adopted by a device or program in the absence of instructions to the contrary by the user.
default directory
A data directory wherein a program seeks certain files such as those associated with its operation or those containing data.
define
To set a value for a symbol or variable.

definition See *resolution.*

defrag, defragment

To reorder a computer disk so that all of the parts of large files are recorded in contiguous clusters. See also, *disk fragmentation.*

degauss

(1) To erase data from a magnetic storage device such as a floppy disk or tape.

(2) To neutralize a magnetic field, such as the buildup of a charge on the screen of a cathode-ray tube monitor.

degradation

A decline in the performance of a computer system as it continues to operate. Such degradation may be short term as during a period of activity when a several programs are opened consuming processor resources which may not be restored completely even after they are closed. These resources are restored, however, when the computer is rebooted. Over time electronic elements can weaken or fail completely causing a permanent form of degradation. Some, such as caused by *fragmentation* can be reversed—see *defrag.*

delete

To erase or cancel, as a block of text or a file.

delimiter

A symbol such as a comma or quotation marks, used to separate elements in a data or *character string.*

descending sort

An alphabetical or numerical arrangement from highest to lowest.

desktop
A group of computer accessory programs that emulate items ordinarily found on a desk, such as a calendar, calculator, or note pad.

desktop computer
A personal or micromini computer small enough to fit on a desk but too large to be easily portable.

desktop publishing
The use of a computer for setting type, creating graphics and special effects, and laying out pages for reproduction.

destination
A data file, directory, computer, or peripheral device to which data is being transmitted.

destructive read
A computer read–out or data transfer that simultaneously erases the source file.

device
Any component, peripheral, technique, or program routine that is a part of a computer system.

device driver
A program or set of programs that interprets instructions for the operation of a peripheral, such as a printer or monitor.

diagnostic
Descriptive of a system or series of routines designed to detect and isolate errors or malfunctions in programs or equipment.

diagnostic message
An error message that describes the source of a problem in a computer, a computer peripheral or in a program.

dialog box
A pane that appears on screen as a part of a program to furnish instructions or information, or to request user input.

dialup
In a computer network, a telephone connection to a host computer or to the network.

digit
A symbol representing an integer in a numbering system, as 0–9 in decimal notation or 0–F in hexadecimal.

digital
Represented by a distinct value, as the *0* or *1* of a binary computer system.

digital camera
A camera that records images in digital format for downloading and viewing on a computer screen.

digital data
Information recorded according to a system of numbers, as binary for the computer.

digital recording
Sound recorded as discrete values.

DIP switch *Dual In–line Package switch*
An integrated circuit that can be programmed with the use of a series of toggle switches.

directory
In a hierarchical file structure, a division that holds related program or data files and sub–directories.

discrete
Of that which is separate and distinct, such as the electronic data elements manipulated by a digital computer.

disk

A computer storage device such as a *fixed disk*, a removable *floppy disk*, or a *CD*.

disk crash

(1) The destruction of a disk and the data it holds as a result of the read/write head coming in contact with the surface of the disk.

(2) Often used to describe any disk failure, such as one that can be corrected by rebooting.

disk drive

The device that contains a computer disk, the mechanism that spins the disk, and that reads from or writes to it.

diskette

A floppy or removable disk.

disk file See *file*.

disk formatting

A process whereby a series of reference points are recorded on a disk in order to allow orderly storage and retrieval of data.

disk fragmentation

A condition that occurs after many reads and writes to a disk in that data for a single file is scattered throughout the disk rather than stored in contiguous sectors.

When a computer file is saved (or rewritten), the system searches for the next open cluster on the disk and writes the data there. If the file requires more than one cluster, the system searches for the next open cluster, records its location, and places data there. Over time, a large file that has been modified can become fragmented and slow down retrieval time if various parts of the file are scattered throughout the disk.

diskless workstation

A network terminal without a disk drive. The terminal is connected to a *file server* that is its sole source of applications and files.

Used in situations where security is of prime concern, the lack of a floppy drive prevents network users from downloading company files. There are, however, a number of disadvantages:

- A shutdown of the entire system if the file server goes down;
- It prevents users from configuring applications to their preferred way of working;
- It precludes installation of *single-user* applications that may be more suitable for certain user's tasks than an application available on the network; and
- It doesn't allow the user to back up his or her own work.

disk pack

A *hard drive* or *fixed disk* that is made up of several individual disks connected by a spindle.

disk sector

A *section* of a disk track.

disk system

All of the elements required for operation of a computer disk including the drive, read/write head or heads, support chip, and driver software.

disk track

One of the concentric circles of a disk where data is stored. See also, *track*.

display console

A screen where the computer user can view data and monitor the operation of a computer.

display resolution See *resolution*.

distortion

A modification of a signal or the view on a monitor screen that produces an undesirable effect.

dithered image

A pattern of black or colored dots that create the image of a full range of gray or color tones on a computer monitor screen.

.DLL *Dynamic Link Library*

Commonly used file name extension for library files used by a program.

DMA *Direct Memory Access*

The transfer of data from *main memory* to a hardware device without passing through the computer's *CPU*. Also called *bus mastering*.

.DOC

File name extension for a *word processor* or information file.

docking station

A "home base" for a laptop or notebook computer. The portable computer is connected to the docking station which provides peripherals such as a CD–ROM drive, and hookups for a printer, mouse, keyboard, and monitor so that the computer can double as a desktop unit.

document

(1) A page of text in a word processor file; a *record* in a database file.

(2) A printed copy of the information contained in a

computer file.

documentation

Information or instructions relating to a peripheral, program, procedure, etc.

document reader

A device that is able to recognize an image on paper and convert it to digital data. A *scanner*.

document retrieval

A system for identifying and retrieving material stored in the computer, often of papers that have been scanned and saved as computer files to save space. See also *archive* (2).

DOS *Disk Operating System*

A proprietary program that controls all of the basic operations of a computer.

dot matrix

A printing technique in which characters are formed by small dots arranged according to patterns established for the characters.

dot pitch

The distance between *phosphor* dots of the same color on the surface of a computer monitor **CRT**. *Dot pitch* is an important consideration when assessing the fineness of computer monitor *resolution*.

double click

To press and release the primary button of a computer *mouse* twice in quick succession. The *double click* is used in programs to perform a variety of tasks, such as to highlight a selection, activate a program, or to call up a document.

double density disk

A type of diskette which can be formatted to compact

data in order to double the disk capacity.

double–sided disk

A diskette which stores data on both sides.

double–speed

Descriptive of a compact disk drive or other device that retrieves data roughly twice as fast as earlier units.

download

The transfer of data to another computer, a peripheral device, or a remote location.

downloadable font See *software font*.

downward compatible

Descriptive of the ability of an upgraded program to run data or formatting created with an earlier version. Also called *backward compatibility*.

dpi

Dots per inch; a measure of the quality of the image from a scanner or output to a printer—the more dots per inch, the finer the image appears to the eye. A *resolution* of 300 dpi is adequate for most tasks as the eye has difficulty discerning any coarseness in an image at that level, although 400 dpi or higher may be required for scanning and **OCR** of small or poorly printed type. Traditionally, 600 dpi and up has been the standard for printing quality graphics, especially *camera–ready copy* for a commercial printing house.

drag

To position the mouse cursor over an item, then press and hold the main mouse button down while moving the cursor thereby moving the image under the cursor.

drag-and-drop

A program feature that allows the moving of an element (see *drag*, above) such as a paragraph of copy or a clip art image between two documents or programs as long as both are visible on the computer screen.

DRAM *Dynamic Random Access Memory*

Memory that must be constantly refreshed to be retained and that is erased when the power is turned off.

draw program

An application for creating artwork or graphics for insertion into a document, spreadsheet, etc. A draw program customarily produces a *vector image*.

drive

The device that causes a disk or tape to move past the read/write head in order to access or store data.

drive designation

The letter assigned to a drive in order to identify it for sourcing by a computer.

driver

A program or routine that translates and conveys messages between a computer and a peripheral device.

drop down menu

A program feature that presents a list of options on screen when a menu title is selected with a mouse or a hot key.

drop cap

The first letter in a paragraph of text that is often embellished and enlarged to extend to the height of two or three lines of the body of the text.

drop height

An expression of the durability of a **removable storage** cartridge; the height from which it can be dropped without suffering significant damage. *Drop height* may sound like a silly consideration, but keep in mind that the cartridges are designed to be carried independent of the computer, sent through the mail, etc.

DSK *Dvorak Simplified Keyboard*

A keyboard in which the letters are arranged to make typing easier and faster. Reportedly superior once it is learned, the Dvorak keyboard will probably never completely replace the more familiar **QWERTY keyboard**.

The *QWERTY keyboard*, modeled after that designed for early mechanical typewriters was not designed with the user in mind so much as to position the letters so that the strikers were less likely to clash when typing rapidly.

DTP See **desktop publishing**.

dual mode printer

A dot matrix printer which has the capability of producing output in a standard computer font at high speeds, or a higher resolution output called **near letter quality** at slower speeds.

dual–scan See **passive**.

dump

To transfer the entire contents of a file to a printer, monitor, or storage device.

Dynamic Data Exchange *DDE*

A type of **link** between documents and applications in which the shared data is updated whenever data

dynamic memory

in the source document is changed; for example, changing information in a spreadsheet will also change any of those spreadsheet cells that are linked dynamically to a document. Not all applications support DDE. Also described as an *automatic link*.

dynamic memory

Memory which must be refreshed constantly in order to preserve the data it holds.

E

EBCDIC *Extended Binary Coded Decimal Interchange Code*

A standard code for numeric representation of alphanumeric characters.

echo

A program command to display information lines on a monitor screen, as of a command that is being executed or data that is being transmitted.

edit

(1) To make changes, as additions or deletions, to a file or document.

(2) A text editor available in newer versions of DOS.

edit command

A program feature that facilitates the process of editing text or graphics, such as *move, copy, cut,* or *paste*.

edit key

Any of the special keyboard keys such as *insert* or *delete* that are used to edit text.

edlin

A line by line text editor available in older versions of DOS. In later versions of DOS, *edlin* has been supplanted by *edit*.

EDP *Electronic Data Processing*
Any manipulation of data by electronic means.

EFT See *Electronic Funds Transfer*.

EGA *Enhanced Graphics Adapter*
An early standard for the display of color on a computer monitor screen.

EIDE *Enhanced IDE*
An upgraded *IDE* interface that provides for the control of larger hard disks (over 528MB) and for faster transfer of data between a computer CPU and a hard disk.

EIS *Executive Information System*
Any software package that permits accessing data from various sources and configuring it according to individual needs.

EISA *Extended Industry Standard Architecture*
A 32–bit bus designed to compete with IBM's *MCA* bus.

electronic bulletin board
A computer message center. See also *Bulletin Board Service*.

electronic funds transfer
The conveyance of money or monetary value by electronic means as for income credited directly to one's bank account or the paying of bills by directing a transfer to a creditor's account without further documentation.

electronic mail See *E–mail*.

electronic spreadsheet
A computer version of a worksheet with data organized in rows and columns.

electrostatic printer
A device that transfers images through the adherence of a toner to charged portions of a receiver; a *laser printer*.

E–mail *Electronic mail*
Correspondence or data transmitted over computer telephone lines. Typically, a letter or memo is composed in a word processing program on the computer off–line then transferred to the recipient via network lines or a service provider.

embed
To place an element or object such as text or graphics from one document, file, or application into another. Embedding implies the inclusion of all data necessary to maintain or change the format of the element within the new application. See also, *link*.

embedded commands
Computer program instructions that establish and maintain the appearance, position and special characteristics of a text or graphics element.

embedded object
A drawing, chart, spreadsheet, sound recording, etc. that is imported from another document or file. The embedded object becomes a part of the host file and may be represented graphically, such as for a drawing or spreadsheet, or it may be reduced to an icon, such as for a sound or video spot. The embedded object is not linked to its source, but may remain linked to the application where it was created so that the source application can be called up from within the host for the object to be edited. See also, *link*, *object linking and embedding*.

embedded pointer
A link between an embedded object and its source file, such as a link between a chart and the spreadsheet from which it was derived.

em dash
A dash (—) that is approximately as long as the height of a particular font, traditionally the width of the letter M.

emulation software
A program that directs a peripheral to imitate another, usually to improve performance, as for the emulation of laser quality output by a dot matrix printer.

enabled
Allowed to operate, as by computer command.

encryption
The jumbling or coding of sensitive data to make it unreadable by another for security purposes.

END
A program code indicating the final command.

en dash
A dash (–) that is approximately half the width of an *em dash*.

End key
A *cursor control key* that directs the cursor to the end of a line of text and, used in conjunction with other keys, to the bottom right of the monitor screen, the bottom of a page, the end of a file, etc.

endless loop See *closed loop*.

end of page indicator
(1) A command embedded in a document to indicate the end of a printed page and the start of a new one.

engine

(2) The sensor on a printer that signals the passage of a sheet of paper.

engine

A processor, as for a computer or printer.

enter

To add information into a computer, as text to a document or records to a database.

Enter

A *function key* used to signal the end of a line, block, or paragraph of copy, or to enable a selected command; also expressed as *CR* or **carriage return** or *Return*.

envelope feeder

A device that attaches to a printer to allow the automatic feeding of envelopes for addressing.

environment

A reference to the type of operating system, peripherals, and programs that make up a computer system.

.EPS *Encapsulated PostScript*

A file name extension used for **PostScript** graphics files and that contain vector or bitmapped graphics information.

equation

An expression of equality, as in an algebraic formula in a computer spreadsheet.

equipment compatibility

The quality of computers and peripherals to share instructions or data.

erase

To delete from computer storage, as a block of copy or a file.

errorlevel
In a program or batch file, a value that is tested to signal a branch.

error message
A message generated by an operating system or program and displayed on a monitor or printer indicating that an error in processing has occurred, often citing the source of the error.

Esc *Escape*
A control function key that halts processing or cancels a command, or in some other way reverts to a former condition, as by backing out of a drop down menu or dialogue box.

escape
To discontinue processing, or to return to a previous menu or operating level.

escape character
The ASCII control character 027 signaled by the Escape key, used in certain program sequences to signal the start of a printer or monitor control code.

Escape key See *Esc*.

escape sequence
A character string prefaced by the escape code (ASCII 027) to flag the computer processor to recognize it as a command.

Ethernet
A local area networking protocol for connection and interaction or communication between computers. See also, *LAN*.

exception system
A management reporting technique in which only those data that vary from the typical or ordinary are

.EXE

highlighted or summarized.

.EXE

The file name extension for an executable file, a program file that is activated when the file name is brought to the *command line* by the user or another program.

execute

To carry out an instruction or set of instructions.

execution

The performance of an operation.

exit

(1) A program branch that returns control to the next higher level.

(2) An *escape* command.

(3) To leave a subroutine and return to the main application program or to leave an application and return to the operating system.

expansion card

A board that is installed in the computer to provide additional memory or functions. Same as an *add-on card*.

expansion slot

A position in the computer housing reserved for the installation of expansion or control boards. Same as a *card slot*.

expression

A symbol or set of symbols that describes a mathematical or logical equation.

extended character set

A set of codes that add additional symbols such as those for forming lines and boxes or special accented characters to the basic ASCII characters.

extended DOS partition See *partition*.
extended VGA See *super VGA*.
external cache
A memory *cache* that is not part of the *CPU*.
external storage
Of a data storage device such as a disk or tape drive that is not contained in the computer console; often one that can be removed and attached to another computer for the transfer or use of data.

extrapolate
To estimate a value based on other known values. For instance, if the cost of manufacturing a product at several different volume levels is known, it may be possible to estimate or predict the cost of manufacturing at other levels.

F

face
All of the styles of a type of a particular design. See also, *font*.
facsimile See *fax*.
fan fold paper
Paper designed for a computer printer in a continuous stream with equally spaced feed holes along a removable strip on each side with perforations between pages and folded accordion-style so as to lie flat.

fast save
An option in some programs that saves only the latest changes to a document. This technique allows saving ones work with a minimum of delay, but tends to use a lot of memory.

FAT See *File Allocation Table*.

fatal error

A malfunction that causes a program or device to cease functioning, usually requiring a reboot.

fault

Any condition that causes a program, peripheral, or the computer itself to cease functioning.

fax *facsimile*

(1) A copy of a document sent to a remote terminal by means of a fax machine or computer modem over telephone lines.

(2) A machine or device used to send and receive such copies.

(3) To send such a copy.

Typically, communication between two stand-alone fax machines involves the scanning of hard copy by the sender and the printing out of a hard copy by the receiver, all in real time, that is to say that both machines are occupied during the time it takes to scan the image, convert the data to signals that can be transmitted over telephone lines, to send the data, to receive and convert it back to digital, then print it out.

A fax machine in a computer is somewhat more flexible, allowing transmission of a document directly from a computer file thus eliminating the scan time. In addition, most modern systems treat a fax transmission as a background event, that is a fax can be sent and received while the computer is otherwise engaged.

The fax that is received is treated as a *graphic element*, whether received as a hard copy or a computer file—the computer file, however, can be read by an **OCR** device and converted to a text file, a real convenience if the document is to be edited.

fax card
A controller board in a computer that enables the transmission and receiving of facsimile images over telephone lines.

FDC See *floppy disk controller*.

feed holes
Small holes along the sides of continuous feed computer paper that engaged by a sprocket wheel for feeding into the printer. Customarily, the strip containing the holes is perforated for easy removal from the printed document.

fetch
To retrieve data or a file from computer storage.

fiber optics
The technique of transmitting light through very thin glass or plastic fibers; often the transmission of data by means of pulses of light.

field See *database field*.

field format
The configuration of a database field such as its size and the type of data it is designed to hold. Database fields are generally formatted to hold a specific type of data such as characters, numbers, or a date in order to reduce the possibility of erroneous entries.

field length
The number of characters in a database field.
The data fields in a database *record* are usually of a fixed length to facilitate control and efficient manipulation of data. Some are dictated by the type of data

field mark

they hold such as a Social Security Number (9 characters excluding the two dashes), a date in *mm/dd/yy* format (8 characters), or a logic field (1 character, for a Y or N) while others are set depending on the need of the user.

A special, memo, or variable length field for holding explanatory text of varying length isn't really a database field; it is a marker that points to a text file.

field mark

A program code that signals the beginning or end of a database field.

field name

The designation that identifies a specific field in a database record, usually descriptive of the data contained in the field.

file

A set of related information, such as for a spreadsheets, database, word processing document, or a program that is identified by a unique name and stored as a unit.

File Allocation Table *FAT*

The system used by DOS to identify and locate files on a disk.

file attribute

The special nature of a file for identification or protection such as read–only, archived, or hidden.

A computer file may be:

• *Read–only* A file that is accessible to the computer or operator, but that cannot be altered; used for program or data files that should not be changed.

• *Archived* An attribute assigned each time a file is

altered and saved; often used for incremental backups—files that have been changed are identified by their archive bit, copied to the backup medium, and the archive bit deleted.

• *Hidden* A designation reserved for critical files that would cause a system shutdown if they were altered or deleted.

file conversion

The transfer or alteration of a file's formatting codes to allow access by a different program.

file extension

A designation comprised of up to three characters following a file name and separated by a period. The extension often aids in identification of the type of file by the operating system, a program, or the user. For example, *.EXE*, *.BAT*, and *.COM* files are recognized by the computer as command files that are executed when the file name is typed on the **command line**; *.DLL* are library files used by a program; *.DOC* and *.TXT* are text files; *.HLP* designates a help file; and *.AVI*, *.BMP*, *.JPG*, *.PCX*, *.TIF*, *.WAV*, are some of the many types of audio and graphics file designations.

Program or executable files of the three types mentioned above do not vary as they rely on the operating system to recognize them for what they are—files written in a language that the operating system can understand and act on. Other files used by a program and data files such as those for documents or graphics are less consistent—programmers may simply use extensions that help them in identifying certain types of files that are of no significance

file locking

outside the program.

Files with common file extensions are not always compatible, such as for the *.DOC* extension that is used by many word processing programs for text files, or the *.TIF* extension that can be used for a number of different tagged image graphic formats.

file locking

Preventing the use of a file by more than one person at a time, a common practice on a network where data files are accessed directly by the uses rather than updated periodically.

file maintenance

(1) The correcting and updating of files and directories to incorporate the most recent data available.

(2) The process of purging the computer storage system of outdated files.

file management

The organization and tracking of files by the operating system, the user, or a software utility.

file manager

A software utility designed to simplify the task of locating and organizing files.

file name

The designation that identifies a specific file.

file name extension See *file extension.*

file protection

(1) A *file attribute* that identifies a file as read–only.

(2) A device on a floppy disk that can be set to make the files on the disk unalterable.

file server

A computer that stores a library of program and data files for a number of users in a network.

file slack
The amount of space allocated for a file on a disk or other storage device that does not contain data; often expressed as a percentage.

file transfer protocol
The rules that govern the transfer of data files within a computer or between two computers.

filter
(1) That which refines output by sifting input according to user– or program–designated criterion.
(2) User input that restricts output to specific information or a group of records in a database, as by selecting fields or specifying a search criterion for particular information in a designated field or fields.
(3) Machine controls that eliminate extraneous and potentially disruptive signals.

financial planning software
A program that assists the user in budgeting, saving, investment or borrowing decisions, etc.

fixed area
A section of storage on a fixed disk that is designated for use by specific files or data and that may not be used by other files or data.

fixed disk
A computer disk that is permanently mounted in the casing with its drive. See also *hard disk*.

fixed length field
A *database field* that is programmed to be of a specific length for all records in the database. See also *field length*.

fixed spacing
Descriptive of type in which every character takes

the same amount of space on a line, such as that
produced by a conventional typewriter. See also,
proportional spacing.

F key See *function key (2)*.

flat file
A *database* that has all of its records contained in a
single file, in contrast to a *relational database*.

flicker
A visible change in the intensity of a monitor display
caused by a slow or uneven *screen refresh*.

flip–flop
An electronic circuit that can be made to assume
one of two stable states, in the computer represented
as 0 and 1.

floppy disk
A removable memory storage device; also called a
diskette.

floppy disk controller
The hardware and software that manages the operation of a floppy *disk drive*.

Floptical
A proprietary system for an external storage medium
that employs laser optics.

flow chart
A graphic representation of the progression through
a series of operations, as of a computer program or
the paperwork in an office.

flush left, flush right
The placement of type that is to be in *alignment*
with the left or right margin, respectively.

FM synthesis
A technique for generating sound in a computer

using *frequency modulation*. See also **wavelength synthesis**.

font

Traditionally descriptive of one typeface and style in one size, such as *Bodoni bold 12 point*. With the introduction of **scalable fonts**, one font often refers to a typeface in a single style but a wide range of sizes. See also **font cartridge**, **software font**.

font cartridge

A small cartridge that connects to a printer and contains information for printing a font or fonts of type in addition to any that are programmed into the printer itself. Font cartridges are a convenient means to add fonts when printing from DOS; **scalable fonts** such as *TrueType®*, are somewhat less expensive and more convenient for printing from *Windows®*.

font generator

(1) Early software for **scalable fonts** that created font files outside an application for downloading to a printer, and **screen fonts** for downloading to an application. Generally expensive and slow, the font generators worked only with a limited number of applications and also subjected the user to the inconvenience of having to select typefaces, styles, and sizes before starting the application in which they were to be used.

(2) The software that creates scalable fonts "on the fly", that is, as they are used.

footer

Printed matter that appears at the bottom of a page and that is usually repeated on every page.

forecasting
The process of seeking to predict future conditions based on a study of past conditions.
Because of its ease of use and speed, the computer has become the tool of choice in business for such things as developing scenarios of the future of a company based on anticipated changes in product mix or manufacturing costs and for developing marketing strategies

foreground
(1) Descriptive of activity that takes place in the view of and usually under the control of the user.
(2) Descriptive of processing that has priority over all other activity.

form
(1) A printed document or computer screen designed for the orderly entry of data.
(2) The configuration or arrangement of data in a report or document.

format
(1) Initializing a disk to accept data.
(2) The system by which data is held in a particular type of file, such as for a spreadsheet or database, or by a particular program.
(3) The layout or arrangement of information in a document.

form design
The fashioning of a screen document for the orderly entry or display of data.

form feed
A command to the printer issued from a computer print program or a control on the printer itself to

automatically advance the paper the length of one form or one page.

formula

A string of symbols that calculate to a value, as in a spreadsheet cell that calls for the total of the values in other specified cells, or that calculates to a logical *true* or *false* as in a **conditional branch** command.

fragmentation

(1) The condition of being broken into parts.

(2) A condition wherein computer files are recorded to scattered rather than contiguous segments on a computer disk.

See also, **defrag**.

frame

(1) An unprinted box that is the placeholder for a block of type, a picture, etc. in a document.

(2) A window on a computer screen that provides a view of information displayed by a program.

friction feed

A type of printer feed similar to that used by a conventional typewrite, used almost exclusively for feeding single sheets.

FTP See **file transfer protocol**.

full screen access

Descriptive of a program feature that allows editing of data anywhere on a computer screen.

Full screen access is common today, but it hasn't always been so. Older programs that were run on mainframes often required that data be entered only from a line near the bottom of the screen—the user specified a line number, entered the data, and then instructed the computer to accept it.

function code

With the advent of the personal computer, the old mainframe mindset remained for a time and programs were transferred largely intact. Those familiar with older versions of DOS with its *edlin* editor or of the *Lotus 1-2-3* spreadsheet program are accustomed to this limited means of data entry. As programmers seek to make the PC more user–friendly, full screen access has became almost universal.

function code

Any symbol or set of symbols that generates an instruction to the computer.

function key

(1) A button on a computer keyboard that is dedicated to a specific task or tasks such as *Enter*, *Page Up*, *Page Down*, *Home*, or *Delete*.

(2) An *F key*; one of a set of ten or twelve keys labeled *F1*, *F2*, etc. that alone or in conjunction with *Ctrl*, *Alt*, or *Shift* are used to execute commands in certain programs.

G

garbage

(1) Descriptive of input or output that has been poorly edited or manipulated, or that is considered unreliable.

(2) Undesirable noise or interference on a transmission line.

gate

(1) A computer chip circuit designed to produce a single output from one or more input signals.

(2) A logic circuit that produces output that varies with its function, such as an AND gate that outputs

a 1 (or True) when both inputs are 1, or an OR gate that produces an output of 1 if either input is 1.

gate array
A set of gates on a computer chip that can be interconnected to perform a distinct function.

GDI *Graphics Device Interface*
The protocol for displaying graphics, including special fonts, on the computer screen.

general purpose computer
A computer that is intended to handle a broad range of applications in contrast to one that is designed for a specific use such as inventory control.

generate
To process or create, as to generate a report from computer data, or to generate a new program.

generation
A class of computer as defined by technological advances. First generation of computers was powered by vacuum tubes, the second generation by transistors, and the third by integrated circuits.

generator
A computer program designed to create other programs or routines for other programs.

GET
A program instruction to fetch data or a file from outside the program or from a non–contiguous source within it.

.GIF *Graphics Interchange Format*
A file name extension for a bitmapped image, a type of graphics file.

gigabyte
One thousand million (one billion) bytes

GIGO

GIGO *Garbage In Garbage Out*
The axiom that the quality of information derived from computer processing is directly related to the quality of the data entered into the computer.

glitch
A malfunction or error, usually of little consequence.

global
Referring to that which applies to a wide range of elements such as: (1) Formatting or instructions that act on all like elements in a computer file; or (2) Formatting that acts on all of the files created by a program or application.

global search
(1) Descriptive of a search through every directory, sub–directory or file on a disk.
(2) A command to find all occurrences of a string in a file, in a group of files, or anywhere on the disk.

global search and replace
A routine that seeks out every incidence of a character string within a file and replaces it with another designated string. For example, a new ZIP code or telephone exchange may require a search for each occurrence of the old number in a database in order to correct those that have changed. In most programs, the user can specify that all replacements are to be made without further input or that the user is to be prompted for each replacement.

glossary
A list of technical or specialized terms. Most computer program manuals contain a collection of terms that pertain generally to the type of application, such as a database or spreadsheet, and especially of

any uncommon terms used or coined by the programmers of the application. For example, a user command to locate files or data within a file may go under the name of *search*, *seek*, or *find*.

GOTO

A program instruction to branch off to a new set of commands. GOTO is described as an **unconditional branch** in that it transfers processing without any testing of conditions.

GPC See *general purpose computer*.

graceful degradation

(1) The process by which an overloaded computer program or system continues to run, albeit less efficiently, allowing the user to shut the system down with minimal loss of files or data.

(2) The process by which a computer system warns of eminent failure to provide for an orderly shutdown. An **uninterruptible power supply** that links a computer to its power source, for example, sounds a warning when power is interrupted and provides auxiliary power to keep the system running for a short time.

graceful exit

The process of closing files and exiting all programs before shutting a computer down. Many programs use temporary files to store instructions and data while the program is running. Disconnecting power while such a program is running can create a collection of temporary or fragmented files that over time can clog storage and degrade performance. In addition, a database file that is terminated without rebuilding its **index** may be corrupted beyond use.

grammar

grammar
The system and structure of a language. In computer programming, grammar is the *vocabulary* or words that are understood in a particular programming language, and the *syntax* or manner in which the words must be used to constitute an executable command.

grammar checker
A program that highlights suspected grammatical or spelling errors, redundancies, etc. in a file or document and suggests alternatives. The grammar checker may be a feature in an application or a separate program to which copy is exported. Some of the more powerful programs check copy according to a style set by the user—formal, informal, technical, etc.—and will "learn" the style of a particular writer so as to avoid highlighting suspected errors that are acceptable to the author.

grandfather file
A computer data file from which two newer files have been formed. In general, when an active file is backed up and the *backup copy* stored, the previous backup or grandfather file becomes superfluous and can be destroyed.

graph
A chart that displays the relative magnitude of associated elements as bars, columns, or sections of a pie.

graphical user interface *GUI*
A computer monitor screen display that simplifies the use of programs and functions by representing them with icons that can be selected with a mouse

or other pointing device.

graphic display

The depiction of graphic elements on a computer monitor screen.

graphic element

Any object saved to a computer file, displayed on a computer monitor screen or printed that is not *alphanumeric*; however, with the advent of *scalable fonts* used in conjunction with *inkjet printers* and *laser printers*, most alphanumerics have become graphic elements as well.

graphics

(1) The representation and manipulation of picture elements as in a *CAD/CAM* or *draw program*.

(2) The process used to display computer data pictorially.

graphics capability

(1) A computer monitor with a graphic interface that permits the depiction of picture elements on screen.

(2) A printer that has the ability to print picture elements.

graphics card

A removable computer circuit board that provides the means for displaying graphics on a monitor screen. It is the graphics card that determines the *resolution* of the display, such as for *VGA* or *super VGA*. Also called a *video card*.

graphics mode

On some *impact printers*, a configuration that allows the printing of *graphic elements* or an *extended character set*, usually programmed with a *DIP switch*.

gray scale
A graduated series of dot patterns used to depict various shades of gray on a computer screen or printout.

grid
(1) A pattern of columns and rows for recording data such as in a spreadsheet.
(2) Two sets of parallel lines running perpendicular to each other as for positioning elements in optical character recognition.

grouping
Arranging data or records in sets based on common attributes.

GUI See *graphical user interface*

gutter
(1) The white space between the printed area and the binding of a book page.
(2) An extra margin provided at the side of a document page to allow for binding; a left-hand or even-numbered page would have a margin on the right side, and a right-hand or odd-numbered page would have an extra margin on the left.

H

hacker
One who has acquired skill in the use of computers, generally for personal pleasure.

halftone
A printed or monitor screen image that creates the impression of varying shades of gray as in a photograph by the use of dots of varying size and density. See also, *continuous tone*.

halt

The untimely termination of computer processing as from a user command or an error in processing.

hand held computer

A computer small enough to be held in the hand, often used to record appointments and addresses, as a spell checker, as a checking account monitor, etc. A hand held computer can be made to interface with a larger computer and used to send data via telephone lines or cellular phone, but of necessity the keyboard is too small for it to be practical for inputting large amounts of data.

handshaking

The protocol for identification and communication between two pieces of equipment.

hanging indent

A text format in which all of the lines in a paragraph are indented except the first. This paragraph is set with a hanging indent.

hang-up

A temporary halt in processing in which the computer no longer recognizes input as from a keyboard or scanner. Frequently the problem is with a single application which can be shut down with a possible loss of some data. Occasionally the problem is more serious and only rebooting can bring operation back to normal.

hard carriage return See *carriage return.*

hard copy

(1) Information or data that is to be input to a computer through a keyboard or scanner.

(2) A printed copy of all or part of a computer file.

hard disk

hard disk
A disk that is mounted with its own drive, usually installed in the computer case.

The *hard disk* is made up of a stack of metal plates, each with a **read/write head** on both sides. The plates are divided into concentric circles called **tracks**. A set of vertical tracks, that is, all those in the same position on each of the plates, is called a **cylinder**. (Think of the cylinders as imaginary tubes or tin cans, all different sizes, set one inside the other, slicing through the stack of plates or disks that hold data.) The track is further divided into **sectors**, the smallest unit of data addressed by the hard disk **controller**.

hard disk controller
The hardware and software that manages the operation of a fixed **disk drive**. The hardware for a personal computer is usually contained in an **add-on card**.

hard error
An equipment malfunction or mistake in processing caused by hardware.

hardware
The computer itself and any of the peripheral devices that are a part of the system.

hardware handshaking
The recognition of and exchange of data between computer hardware devices. See also **handshaking**.

hardware resources See **resources**.

hard-wired
Of permanently connected circuits that cannot be altered by programming.

hash
(1) Useless output.
(2) Computer output that has been corrupted by a
hardware or software malfunction or by a programming error.

head
(1) The read/write head in a disk drive.
(2) The device on an impact or ink jet printer that
transfers characters to paper.

head crash
A circumstance in which the read/write head comes
into contact with the surface of a disk. A head crash
is catastrophic for both the disk drive mechanism
and the disk itself and almost always results in a
complete loss of data.

header
Printed matter such as a title, page number, etc. at
the top margin of a document or report that usually
repeats on every page.

head gap
The space between a read/write head and the surface of a disk or other magnetic medium.

heat sink
A device that attaches to some computer chips to
absorb excess heat generated by the chip, thereby
promoting more efficient operation of the circuits
and extending the life of the chip.

help
A program feature that provides guidance to the
user, explaining the meaning of commands or formatting options, instructions for performing various
tasks, etc. See also, *context sensitive help*.

help screen

help screen
A separate window on screen that provides guidance
for the user. The help screen is often interactive, allowing a selection of subjects about which the help
program offers information.

hertz, Hz
One cycle per second.

heuristic
Of a problem–solving technique that involves selecting the best of several solutions to a problem, then
using what is learned in succeeding steps of a program.

hexadecimal
A numbering system in base sixteen used in computer notation. Hexadecimal digits are represented
as 0 through 9 and A through F.

hierarchical
(1) Referring to a system in which elements are arranged in order of rank.
(2) In the computer, a system of directories and files
wherein the *root directory* is of the highest order
and contains all of the subordinate directories and
subdirectories that contain program and data files.
In a multi–user system or one that is used to store a
large and varied assortment of files, the directory
structure plays a key role in efficient operation.
Commonly, program or application files are stored in
a second–level directory, that is, a directory one level
under the root directory. Data files may be organized
in a number of ways, but they should be grouped in
directories according to some common attribute:
• An application may have all of its files saved to a

single subdirectory called DATA, or to several subdirectories named for users or projects.

• Conversely, one might set up second-level directories by user or project and save data files in the appropriate directories without regard to the application in which they were created. In addition, each second-level directory may be broken down into subdirectories by user or project. A large project may be further broken down into subdirectories—a newsletter for example may have its own directory with subdirectories for each issue.

All of this may sound overly systematized, but it doesn't take much searching for an important document of uncertain name somewhere on a two gigabyte hard drive to make a believer of anyone.

high level language

A programming language in which the commands and syntax are somewhat similar to a spoken language. Working in such a language precludes the need for the programmer to have a knowledge of *machine language*. Writing code for complex program routines is more efficient in a high level language as a single command may replace several commands in machine language. Changes made at a later date also require less effort because of the ease in which one can read the program and follow the original logic.

highlighted

(1) An element on the computer monitor screen that is set apart from others by underlining, reverse video, or contrasting color.

(2) A reference to a block of copy or a graphic

element that has been selected for some purpose such as to copy or move it.

high order language See *high level language*.

high resolution See *resolution*.

high speed storage

Of a removable data storage device that offers fast *access time* that is comparable to that of an installed hard drive.

hit

An accurate match, as of a character string in a database search.

hit ratio

(1) A measure of the number of incidences in which a program or routine is successful in completing its task compared to the total number of times it is called on to perform the task. The *hit ratio* of an **OCR program**, for example, expresses its effectiveness in correctly recognizing and recording the characters in a scanned file.

(2) An indication of the effectiveness of a memory cache. The hit ratio is expressed as a percentage derived by dividing the number of times a call for data was found in the cache versus the total number of calls.

HLL See *high level language*.

.HLP

File name extension for a *help* file.

home

Any of several starting positions for the cursor on a computer monitor screen, such as the beginning of a line, the beginning of a paragraph, the top left of the screen, the top of the page, or the beginning of a file.

home computer
A computer designed for home use.
Originally envisioned as a small inexpensive system less powerful than a business computer, there is now little difference between the home and office computers. In fact, for many, the system they use at home can outperform the one used in the office. Several factors have served to transform the home computer from one designed simply for playing games and for personal software, such as an address book, checking account, etc. to a system that rivals the office machine:

• Technological advances and falling prices have placed very powerful computers within the reach of the household budget.
• The world–wide web has become a consumer-oriented facility, allowing the user to search out information on virtually any subject and to chat with 'neighbors' around the world.
• CD–ROM drives open the door to the vast collections of data available on CD's. A CD not only takes up a lot less space than a 20 volume set of encyclopedias but it's easier and more fun to use.
• New powerful games with enhanced graphics and sound often require a computer more powerful than one needed for most office applications.

Home (key)
A cursor movement key that sends the cursor to the beginning of a line of text and, depending on the program and in conjunction with other keys, to any of several other positions such as the top left of the screen or the beginning of a file.

home security system

A combination of hardware and software designed to monitor such things as lights, smoke detectors, and windows and doors.

hopper

A tray that holds single sheets of paper for feeding into a printer.

host

The home or controlling computer in a network of computers or printers.

hot key

A key combination that executes a macro or command that would otherwise require several key strokes.

hot line

A telephone number provided by an equipment or software manufacturer, or a dealer through which a user may access technical assistance.

hot swap

The ability to mount or dismount a *PCMCIA card* peripheral without shutting down the computer.

housekeeping

(1) The process of deleting old files, arranging files in their proper directories, and maintaining an orderly file structure for efficient operation. See also, *hierarchical*.

(2) An exiting procedure performed by a program when it is shut down, such as indexing and closing files and deleting temporary files.

hub

In a local computer network, the common connecting point for terminals in a *star* configuration. Also called a **concentrator**.

hyperlink

A program device that connects computer documents or applications and that provides for rapid switching from one to another.

hypertext

A database system the provides links between text, sound, video, and graphics which provides the means to change seamlessly back and forth or to combine them.

Hz See *hertz*.

I

IC See *integrated circuit*.

icon

A graphic image on a computer screen that represents a directory, file, utility, etc., and that can be selected with a mouse click.

IDE *Integrated Drive Electronics*

A commonly used standard for transferring data between a computer CPU and a hard drive. See also, *SCSI, EIDE*

IDP See *Integrated Data Processing*.

IF, IF statement

A **reserved word** in a **conditional branch** specifying that when (IF) a condition exists, the first set of instructions is to be followed and that when (IF) the condition does not exist, a different set of instructions is to be followed. Also called *IF THEN ELSE*.

The *IF statement* is used extensively in spreadsheet and database formulas. For example, one may use a spreadsheet to calculate sales commissions. In this

illegal character

illustration commission are paid at the rate of 10% on all sales, but only if sales are over $500. Thus:

Statement:

If (salesperson#1 sales) are greater than 500, **then** (salesperson#1 sales) times 10%, **else** 0

and, assuming that salesperson #1's sales are contained in cell A1 of a spreadsheet, the formula may be written as:

Formula:

IF (*A1*) > 500 THEN (*A1*)*.1 ELSE 0

Note that * is the multiplication symbol in computer formulas.

The *syntax* must of course be correct for the program. Some programs use the reserved word IF with the rest of the formula written in parenthesis, as:

Formula:

IF(A1 > 500,*A1*.1,0)

with the words ELSE and THEN replaced by commas.

illegal character

A character or symbol that is unacceptable in a specific situation, such as: (1) a symbol not available in a particular type font; or (2) a letter entered in a database number field.

illegal instruction

A command in a program formula that is not a *reserved word* in that particular program.

image editing, image enhancement

Altering, improving, or combining graphic images

such as art or photographs by use of a computer
program. High end software provides the greatest
flexibility and ease of use by *layering*, that is, placing
each graphic element on a separate layer so that
changing one image does not alter another.
imaging
To create or modify a graphic representation with
the use of a computer program such as a paint or
draw program.
impact printer
A printer that creates an image by striking an inked
ribbon that transfers an image to the paper or other
carrier.
inclusive
Incorporating as part of the whole, such as the part
of a formula in which terms or values joined by the
reserved word *AND* must both be considered in
evaluating the formula.
incremental backup
A backing up or copy of a portion of the computer
files present, usually only those that have been
changed since the last backup. An *incremental
backup* is most practical when only a limited number of the files on a computer are accessed regularly
and precludes the need for copying all of the program and data files on a computer. Even with incremental backups It is a good practice to back up
the entire computer every few months or so.
index
(1) An alphabetized list of programs, documents, or
features.
(2) A file that holds instructions for sorting and

accessing records in a database. A database of names and addresses, for example, may be indexed on last names to facilitate finding a particular record, and on zip codes to select records for a regional mailing.

indexed sequential access method

A method of storing database records sequentially, or as they are entered, and retrieving them in any order desired by use of an index. See *index (2)*.

induction

The generation of an electrical charge or magnetic field in a conductor when placed in proximity to a charged body—the means by which a *read/write head* charges a *flip-flop*.

information

Any data that can be stored, retrieved and manipulated by a computer.

information management

The systems and techniques involved in effectively compiling and manipulating useful data.

information processing

The manipulation of compiled data and the preparation of reports from the data.

information retrieval

Descriptive of the techniques for storage and accessing of data from storage in the form or pattern that the user desires.

.INI

File name extension for a *configuration* file.

initialize

(1) To format a computer disk to accept data.

(2) To boot up a computer by loading the system files

it needs to become functional.

ink jet printer

A printer that forms images from tiny jets of ink spayed on the paper or other receiver.

in–line processing

The processing of data as it is entered, such as for recording sales with a *bar code* reader or recording times from a *shop floor collection* system.

input

Information entered into a computer or peripheral from the keyboard, a disk or other memory device, or from an external source such as a telephone line.

input buffer

An area of computer memory that accepts and temporarily stores data for transfer to its destination. The input buffer serves to compensate for differences in transmission speeds among various devices and provides for the transfer of data without interruption to other processing.

input device

Any equipment linked to the computer that is an entry point for data, such as a keyboard, an optical scanner, or a modem.

input limited

Of a computer or program that is limited by the speed at which input data is processed, such as a *bar code* scanner.

input/output *I/O*

A reference to the conventions for transmitting data between a computer and its peripherals, or to an external device.

input/output buffer, I/O buffer See *input buffer*.

input/output bus, I/O bus See *bus* (1).

inquiry routine

The technique for seeking and selecting specific records from a database. Inquiry routines vary depending on the program in which the database was created.

installation

(1) The process of setting up and configuring a computer system or program.

(2) All of the hardware and software that makes up a computer system.

installed

(1) Of a peripheral connected to a computer and integrated into its system.

(2) Of software that has been copied to a fixed disk and that is operating properly.

instruction

A command to a computer to set a parameter, execute an operation, etc.

instruction code

The vocabulary of *selected words* that are understood by a particular computer or program.

instruction format

The syntax required by a particular program for issuing a command to a computer.

integrated circuit

An electronic device that contains a number of circuit elements and interconnections.

integrated data processing

Computer processing that blends and synchronizes the operation of various elements of the system for greatest productivity.

integrated software

(1) A set of applications that are able to share data.

(2) A program package that offers a combination of features, such as word processor, spreadsheet, and database capability.

integrated system

A combination of computers and peripherals that work together.

intelligence

See *artificial intelligence*, *adaptive system*.

intreactive processing

Computer processing that requires input from the user at certain points in the procedure.

interactive program

An application that responds to each user command as it is entered, then waits for the next command.

interactive system

A computer system that provides a means of communication between the operating system and the user or peripherals.

interface

Hardware or software that forms a link between devices and allows them to communicate with each other.

interlaced

Descriptive of a *refresh* routine for a computer screen that involves scanning every other line on each pass. Interlacing conserves resources and provides a faster refresh, but usually causes a flicker. See also, *non-interlaced*.

interleaving

A routine that directs the computer to switch

between applications, thus appearing to run both at the same time, such as printing in the background while accepting new data entered in the foreground.

internal storage

Data storage that is built into, and directly accessible by, the computer CPU.

Internet

A worldwide network of computer systems.

interrupt

(1) A control signal that directs the computer to halt processing on one level and move to another.

(2) A cessation of processing caused by an error in a program or the computer system.

interrupt priority

The order of precedence in which signals are processed, for example, input from the keyboard usually has priority over background printing.

interrupt request *IRQ*

The traffic cop of the computer world that directs the transmission of data between devices.

Maintaining orderly communications between a computer's CPU and its hardware devices requires constant checking to determine when a device needs service, opening a line of communication, and keeping the line clear of interference by other devices that need attention. To this end, devices are assigned IRQ lines controlled by a special chip that is constantly scanning (or **polling**) to determine who needs attention. When it is established that there is data to be sent to or received from a device, the **controller**, in effect, opens the proper channel, allows data to be transferred, then moves on.

See also, *interrupt priority*.

inventory control program

A system for creating an accounting of goods in inventory by adjusting for additions and withdrawals, often in conjunction with accounts receivable and accounts payable so that the quantity and value of inventory is adjusted with each transaction.

I/O See *Input/Output*.

I/O buffer

A portion of memory dedicated to the temporary storage of data received or to be sent by the computer—the buffer compensates for differences in communication speeds between devices and prevents the interruption of other operations.

I/O bus

A set of lines that carries signals between devices within the computer system.

I/O port

The physical connector between a computer and its peripherals.

IRQ See *interrupt request*.

ISA *Industry Standard Architecture*

A bus designed for the PC introduced in the early 1980's and upgraded a few years later to a 16–bit bus, the old standby, still common in most personal computers.

ISAM See *indexed sequential access method*.

italic

Originally a style of type modeled on a Renaissance script, like this sentence. In this day, any font of type in which the letters are slanted to the right, generally used for emphasis.

iterate

To say or do again, such as a program search command that is repeated numerous times with different values.

iteration

The technique of repeating a set of program instructions to achieve desired results. This is accomplished by referencing a counter in the routine and adding one for each repetition until a certain number is reached or a certain condition is met.

J

job

A task or series of tasks to be accomplished by the computer.

job cost system

A computer program designed to account for the cost of labor and materials associated with the manufacturing of a specific product or a quantity of that product.

job entry system

(1) A procedure whereby data relative to a manufacturing process, such as materials requisitioned and labor expended, are recorded for later evaluation.

(2) The procedure for setting up the computer to perform a task or series of tasks.

job processing

The execution of a particular task or series of tasks by the computer.

joystick

A device that can be attached to the computer to control the action of a game on the monitor screen.

.JPG *JPEG, Joint Photographic Experts Group*
File extension for a special compression format used to store photographs.

Julian date
A calendar date expressed as a five digit number—the first two digits represent the year followed by three digits that represent the number of the day of the year. A date thus expressed can be used in calculations that involve intervals of time.

jumper
A type of switch used to set the configuration for a computer card or device.

justify
To space text so that it is lined up at both side margins; also called *full justify*.

justify left, justify right See *flush left, flush right*.

K

K *Kilo*
One thousand. In binary numbers, used to express 2^{10} or 1024.

KB, kb *Kilobyte*
One thousand bytes, or more specifically, 1024 bytes.

kerning
Proportional spacing between typeset characters. Generally, type should be set so that the amount of white space between each of the characters is relatively equal.

keyboard
A panel of buttons containing the alphabet, numbers, and various symbols serving as one of the

keyboard buffer

primary devices for entering data into a computer.

keyboard buffer
A memory cache that holds keystrokes as they are entered and prior to being processed. Commonly, when computer processing is slowed for any reason, the keyboard buffer will hold a finite number of characters or commands as they are entered from the keyboard until the CPU catches up and acts on the keystrokes. Note that certain types of processing, depending on the application, may lock out the keyboard so that anything entered is ignored during the processing. Also called a *type ahead buffer*.

keyboard control key See *control key*.

keyboard lockout
(1) A program feature that prevents entry from the keyboard while the computer is processing data.
(2) A hardware or software security system that prevent use of the keyboard and thus denies access to the computer by unauthorized users.

keypad
A small, special purpose keyboard with a limited number of buttons. A separate number keypad is often used in conjunction with a laptop or notebook computer as most lack a number pad.

keystone distortion
Distortion of the image on a computer screen when the top and bottom edges of the image are out of square.

key word
A word or words in a formula that indicate the operation to be performed.

KHz See *kilohertz*.

kilobyte *KB, kb*
Approximately one thousand bytes; specifically 2^{10} or 1024 bytes.
kilocycle *kc*
Kilohertz; one thousand cycles per second
kilohertz *KHz*
One thousand cycles per second.

L

label
A name or designation that identifies a computer disk, a file, program routine, or range of cells in a spreadsheet.
LAN *Local Area Network*
Two or more computers that are linked within an office or a building to share programs, data, output devices, etc.
language
A precise system of vocabulary and syntax for writing programs; *absolute* or *machine* language refers to instructions that can be understood directly by the computer; an *artificial* or *high level* language more closely emulates spoken English to make programming and revisions easier.
laptop computer
A portable computer complete with an integrated screen and keyboard. Although there is no firm definition of what constitutes a *laptop* other than portability, it is generally smaller in size than a desktop computer and larger than a ***notebook computer***. The laptop is more likely than a notebook to have a keyboard that nearly approximates the size of

laser

one used on a desktop.

laser *Light Amplification by Stimulated Emission of Radiation*

A device that emits intense light of a precise wavelength.

laser disk

A compact storage disk that is written to and read from using laser technology.

laser printer

An electrostatic printer that uses laser technology to create images on paper or other carrier, such as film.

laser scanner

A device using laser technology to copy and convert images into digital data.

layer

The third dimension in a three dimensional array.

LBA *Logical Block Addressing*

A technique for addressing data on a computer disk in which sectors are numbered consecutively for identification and retrieval. See also, **CHS**.

LCD *Liquid Crystal Display*

A computer screen that uses liquid crystals to create an image. See also, *active matrix*, *passive matrix*.

leader

(1) In typesetting, a series of symbols joining two character strings, often periods, dashes or a line.

(2) A symbol depicted by a set of three closely set dots (...) usually representing an incomplete expression.

LED *Light–Emitting Diode*

A semiconductor diode that converts electrical

current to light, used in digital displays such as for a calculator or clock.

left justified
Type aligned along the right margin of a document.

letter quality
Representative of characters printed on a typewriter, a measure of the relative quality of the image from a computer printer.

level
(1) The separation or division of otherwise similar elements, as the level of a directory in the hierarchical structure.
(2) Denoting relative position in value, performance, etc.

library
A collection, as of programs, databases, computer graphics, etc.

light pen
A photosensitive device connected to a computer that can alter data, activate commands, etc. through the display monitor. Also called *electronic stylus*.

light sensitive
Descriptive of a material that reacts to the stimulus of light.

limiting
Descriptive of a device that because of its slower speed or capacity restricts processing.

line feed
A command to the printer to advance the paper one line.

line spacing
(1) The distance between the baselines of two lines of

type, calibrated in inches, points, or picas.

(2) The number of lines per inch on a printed page.

line voltage

Power supplied by a local utility company.

link

(1) A connection between two computers or a computer and its peripherals.

(2) A connection between data contained in a document and the computer file or application from which it was copied.

Linking capabilities and the links themselves vary from one application to another: some provide an *automatic link* such as through **Dynamic Data Exchange** that updates data in the host document whenever the source document is changed; others require that the user stipulate when data is to be updated.

See also **object linking and embedding**.

linked documents

Records or files that are connected so that data or formatting from one can be automatically entered in another, such as billing records that are automatically added to an accounts receivable file.

liquid crystal display See **LCD**.

load

To call up a program or data to the computer's main memory from a storage device.

local bus

A technique that provides a direct link between a computer's CPU and peripherals such as a video card or hard disk controller.

locate See **global search**.

lockout
(1) Denial of access to a computer by some type of security system.
(2) In a program, temporary denial of access to commands during processing.

log
A record of times and dates that a computer or program is accessed by each user, usually including the duration of use.

logic
(1) Correct or valid reasoning.
(2) The use of symbols in a formula to test the relationship between elements.
(3) Non–arithmetic processing such as sorts and searches that calculate to a yes or no.

Logical Block Addressing *LBA*
A technique for addressing data on a computer disk in which sectors are numbered consecutively for identification and retrieval; used mainly by **SCSI** controllers. See also, **CHS**.

logical drive See *partition*.

logic circuit
Computer circuitry that controls logic functions.

logic formula
A group of symbols that calculates to a logical *true* or *false*, as for a conditional branch.

logic operator
Any of the selected words or symbols used in logic formulas.

log in, log on
To type a password or other information that allows access to a computer or program.

lookup table

lookup table
A set of variables arranged in a two dimensional array. As an adjunct to a spreadsheet, the lookup table is used to locate the value of a variable called for from a cell formula.

loop
A set of program instructions that are executed until a specific condition is met. See also, **closed loop**.

loop ender
A value expressed in a loop instruction to signal a branch and prevent unnecessary iterations of the loop.

loop feedback
The output value that modifies input for the next iteration of a loop instruction.

loosely coupled
Descriptive of computers that are connected, but that are capable of independent operation.

M

machine dependent
Of an operating system or program that can only function on a specific computer or a specific type of computer.

machine error
A program error caused by an equipment malfunction.

machine instruction
A computer instruction coded so that it can be understood and acted on directly by the computer.

machine language
(1) The set of binary signals that can communicate

directly with a particular type of **CPU**.

(2) The language into which a high level language command must be translated or compiled to allow a particular processor to act on it.

machine learning

The process by which a program records the result of a computation or action and then uses that result to modify future computations or actions.

See also, **adaptive system**.

machine readable

Of characters or symbols, such as a **bar code**, that can be read directly into a computer by means of an input device such as a scanner.

machine word See **computer word**.

macro

A set of instructions that are executed by a single command or by means of a hot key or shortcut key combination. Macros are commonly used to simplify the accomplishment of repetitive tasks that would otherwise require a number of individual steps.

Macros are used extensively by programmers to provide special features in some programs such as a key combination that formats copy.

Many applications also provide a guide to the program's **macrocode** to allow the user to create macros of his or her own choosing; some have a 'record' feature that enables the user to produce a macro by demonstrating the keystrokes that are to make up the macro.

macro code, macrocode

(1) The language in which a macro is written.

(2) The set of instructions that make up a macro

macro library
A collection of macros available to the user from within a particular program.

macro recorder
A program feature that allows the recording of keystrokes for incorporation in a macro.

magnetic card
(1) A small card such as a *PCMCIA card* that is used to store magnetic data.
(2) A card with a *magnetic strip* attached, such as for holding credit information or medical data.

magnetic disk
(1) A device for storing computer data.
(2) A *hard disk* or a *floppy disk*.

magnetic ink character recognition See *MICR*.

magnetic ink scanner
A device for reading special characters printed with magnetic ink. See also, *MICR*.

magnetic strip
A small ribbon of material used to store digital data, usually applied to a portable device such as a credit card.

A magnetic strip may contain only permanent data such as a credit card number that can be read by machine or it may have the ability to receive changing data such as a credit limit. Interactive cards are increasingly being used as 'cash cards' that are assigned a fixed cash value with each purchase deducted directly from the card's memory.

magnetic tape
A medium for the storage of computer data, used mainly for backing up a computer system.

magnitude
The size of a number or value regardless of its sign.

mail merge
A program feature that combines names, addresses, and other data from a database with a body of prepared text.
Mail merge may be used to send letters to a client database or to a group selected from a database. A reminder to delinquent accounts may be linked to an accounts receivable database so as to include the amount that is past due in the letter.

mainframe
A large computer, usually designed to serve a number of remote terminals.

main memory
The internal memory of a computer (**RAM**) from which programs are run.

management information system
A company or organization's facilities for gathering, storing, and managing data for use in decision making.

manual link
A connection between elements in a document or file that is updated only at the command of the user. See also, *automatic link*.

manufacturer's software
A system program or driver that is supplied by a manufacturer for the operation of their hardware.
Computer programs designed to interact with hardware devices such as a printer or sound card usually come with device driver software; however, manufacturer's software that can be installed when such a

117

device is added is designed to take better advantage of the device's full range of capabilities.

margin

(1) The outer limits of a body of copy on a page.

(2) The unprinted area around a block of copy.

marginal

In a word processing application, a reference to text or graphics that are positioned outside the normal printed area of a block of copy. A marginal may, for example, be an explanatory note, a section header placed in the margin of a document or extending out into the margin, or it may be a masthead running along the side margin instead of at the top of a newsletter.

marker

A reference point within a document or file that can be quickly accessed, such as a *bookmark*.

mask

(1) A pattern of bits used in *search* operations.

(2) A pattern or matrix used for comparison, as in *optical character recognition*.

master

(1) A template or formatted document to which variable data is entered.

(2) A primary or main file, such as of a database, to which data is entered only after it has been verified.

math coprocessor

An *integrated circuit* that works in conjunction with a computer's *CPU* to perform high speed arithmetic calculations.

At one time a math coprocessor was a separate chip that could be added to the computer; most modern computers incorporate the circuitry into the CPU.

mathematical operator
A symbol that governs an arithmetic computation, as + (add), – (subtract), × or * (multiply), and ÷ or / (divide).

matrix
(1) A pattern for the comparison of elements in optical character recognition; an acceptable likeness of an image to a character matrix prompts the program to enclode the image as an alphanumeric character.
(2) A two dimensional *array*.

MB, mb See *megabyte*.

MCA *Micro Channel Architecture*
An advanced 16–bit and 32–bit bus developed by IBM to replace the ISA bus.

medium
An instrument or means by which something is accomplished, such as for magnetic disks or tapes that are *computer storage media*, or or for sight and sound that are *mediums of communication*.

media
Plural for *medium*. See also, *multimedia*.

megabyte *MB, mb*
One million bytes.

megahertz *MHz*
One million cycles per second.

memory
(1) *Volatile memory* that is erased when power is shut down; the area in a computer or printer where data is held during processing.
(2) *Static memory* such as on a hard or floppy disk; that part of a computer where programs and data

are stored.

memory allocation

The designation of a precise location in memory for a particular function such as *input/output* functions or a *swap file*.

memory card

(1) A computer *add-on card* that provides additional storage, usually slower to access than a *hard disk*.

(2) A *PCMCIA card*.

(3) A credit card or similar device that contains a *magnetic strip* or chip for storing specific data.

memory manager

A device or technique for controlling the way in which memory operates.

memory map

A graphic representation of the location of devices loaded into memory.

memory mapping See *memory allocation*.

memory resident

Descriptive of a program or utility that is loaded in RAM, ready to be called up at any time.

menu

A list of options that can be called up and selected by a user, contained within a computer application.

menu-driven

Descriptive of a computer program that offers menus from which the user can select options for formatting or processing.

merge

(1) To combine, as two or more files or sets of database records into a single file or database.

(2) To combine elements of two or more files or sets of database records to create a new file or output. See *mail merge*.

merged sort
To combine and arrange two or more sets of database records in a particular order, such as alphabetically.

message See *error message*.

MHz See *megahertz*.

MICR *Magnetic Ink Character Recognition*
A system for recording data from symbols printed with magnetic ink. This is the means used by the banking industry to read and record checking account transactions; the numbers printed along the base of a bank check are MICR symbols.

microcomputer
A small computer driven by a single integrated circuit and designed for use by one person. Also called a *PC*.

microprocessor
A chip that is the central processing unit for a microcomputer.

.MID
File extension for data conforming to the protocol for interaction between digitized musical instruments and a computer.

MIDI See *musical instrument digital interface*.

MIDI adapter
Hardware that provides communication between a computer and a sound device.

MIDI–compatible sound device
An instrument such as a keyboard or synthesizer

minicomputer

that can be used to record and play back sound through a computer.

minicomputer

A computer smaller than a **mainframe** and larger than a **microcomputer**, intended to support multiple users.

MIS See **Management Information System**.

mnemonics

(1) Memory aids.

(2) Computer program commands designed to make remembering their function easier, as *Q* for *quit*, or *P* for *print*.

MOD See **modulo**.

modem *MOdulator/DEModulator*

A device for translating digital signals to telephone signals and back, used for communicating between computers via telephone lines.

modular

Descriptive of a computer program that is made up of a series of routines, each intended to perform a special task.

module

A device or program element that is part of a larger whole, designed to run on its own or in conjunction with other elements to perform a specific function.

modulo *MOD*

A program command that returns the remainder of a division.

moiré

An undesirable wavy pattern of color caused by misalignment of dots on a printed document or of pixels on a color monitor screen.

MOL *Machine Oriented Language*
A computer programming language that is intended
for use with a specific computer or type of computer.

monitor
A display screen that permits viewing the user's interaction with a computer.

monochrome
A computer screen display in one color or shades of
one color. More effective for mobile computing than a
color display screen, monochrome costs and weighs
less, and offers better battery life.

monospacing See *fixed spacing*.

morphing *morphogenesis*
The formation and alteration of structures with the
aid of a computer. For the non-scientific user,
morphing generally refers to a program that allows
the altering and combining of images such as those
of a person or animal.

MOS *Metal Oxide Semiconductor*
A type of integrated circuit.

motherboard
The primary circuit board in a computer.

mouse
A hand-held device which when moved on a flat surface moves the cursor on a computer screen. The
mouse is equipped with at least one button that is
used to position the cursor or select (*click*), *drag-
and-drop*, and *double-click*. In addition, it may
have one or two *programmable buttons* used to
perform special tasks .

move
A command that copies text or a graphic element to

moving average

a new location and deletes the original.

moving average

A statistical average derived from a set of data which is updated by deleting the oldest elements as new elements are added. A twelve month average of sales and profits for a company, for example, is maintained by adding a thirteenth month's figures, then deleting the first month's figures and recalculating the average.

.MPG *MPEG, Motion Picture Experts Group*

File extension for compressed video data.

MSCDEX

A Microsoft program that assigns a drive letter to a *CD-ROM* drive.

multilevel processing

A condition in which a user interacts with a computer while other processing takes place out of the view of the user. The secondary processing may be related to the program being run or it may be outside the program.

multimedia

Descriptive of the ability to embed a combination of sight and sound elements in a computer program, such as a section of video tape or sound in a text document.

multiplexer

A system that manages signals between two or more devices simultaneously.

multiscan monitor

A computer monitor that provides for setting the screen *refresh* to a variety of rates in addition to the the 60 Hz standard.

multitasking
The ability of a CPU to execute two or more programs or routines at the same time, either by independent processing or by *interleaving*.

multi-user system
A computer system designed to manage input and output from several terminals at the same time.

musical instrument digital interface
The protocol for interaction between digitized musical instruments and a computer.

N

name
A designation that identifies a *directory*, a *file*, a *database field*, a spreadsheet range, etc.
Commonly, a directory or database field is given a name that clearly identifies its content. A data file may have a name that references content, or it may be identified by a combination of letters and numbers. Some spreadsheet programs allow for the naming of a range of cells so that those frequently used in formulas can be called up by their range name rather than the cell location, such as *SUM(MAYSALES)* instead of *SUM(C3:C12)* to call up the total of sales for May.

native
Indicative of origin; that is, the application, format, or programming language in which a set of data was created.

native language
The *machine language* that is used to communicate with a particular type of microprocessor.

natural language

natural language
  A spoken dialect or reasonable facsimile that is not understood directly by a computer.

near letter quality *NLQ*
  A designation of the ability of a printer to emulate the quality of a typewriter.

nest, nesting
  The placing of a program or data element inside another program or data element, such as an **IF statement** in which a second condition is tested after the first tests positive.
  For example, the formula,

  IF(SALES>1000,SALES*.10,IF(SALES>500,SALES*.05,0))

  calculates that "If sales are greater than $1000, a 10% commission is earned, whereas if sales are greater than $500, a 5% commission is earned, and, by default, if sales are less than $500, no commission is paid. Note that the second IF statement is 'nested' within the first and that each IF statement is enclosed in brackets. The number of elements that can be nested is limited only by the length of the formulas allowed within a program.

netBIOS *Network Basic Input/Output System*
  The protocol used by Microsoft's computer network operating system.

network
  A number of computers and peripherals interconnected so as to share information and resources. A network may be made up of computers, printers, scanners, or other devices.

network server
  A computer that stores and manages programs,

data, and peripherals such as output devices for other computers and workstations connected through a network. Also called a *file server*.

new–line character
A printer control character that moves a printer head or printer program to a new line. Also called a *line feed*.

NIC *Network Interface Card*
A PC card that provides a connection to a computer network.

NLQ See *near letter quality*.

node
Any of the terminals or workstations connected to a computer network.

noise
Any faulty element in a transmission. Commonly, *noise* comprises extraneous material in a computer file caused by poor translation of formatting when importing data from a foreign program, a faulty connection that causes garbled data when receiving over telephone lines, or random dots picked up by a scanner.

non breaking hyphen
A hyphenation symbol in a word processing program that prevents the dividing of a hyphenated word at the end of a line, used especially for a hyphenated name.

nonbreaking space
A special symbol in a word processing program that prevents two words from being separated. If the words fall at the end of a line of copy and don't fit, they both fall to the next line; used mostly to

facilitate understanding, when the separation of words in the text might cloud their meaning.

nondestructive read
The accessing of a computer file while maintaining a copy of the file in storage.

When a computer file is opened, the contents are made accessible to the user. Any changes to the file are held in *temporary storage* until the file is saved to a disk or tape. Customarily the file is saved with the same file name so that the new data overwrites the old. If the file is saved with a new name, the old data is retained in the old file. Some programs automatically create a backup copy of the old file with a different *file extension* each time a newer version is saved. See also, *destructive read*.

non-erasable
Descriptive of a file or storage device that is *read-only*, that is, the data it contains can be accessed by the user, but it cannot be altered.

non-interlaced
Descriptive of a *refresh* routine for a computer monitor screen that involves scanning lines sequentially on each pass. Non-interlacing requires more resources and provides a slower refresh, but usually offers an improved image over an *interlaced* screen.

nonprinting character
A command or formatting control character that modifies an image as drawn on a computer screen or as output to a printer, but that does not appear as a distinct readable character.

NOT
An exclusive operator used in programming such as

for a spreadsheet formula.

notation

A combination of *symbols*, *reserved words*, etc. used to designate a computer command.

notebook computer

A portable computer with an integrated screen and keyboard contained in a single unit. The notebook generally is smaller and lighter than a laptop (especially noteworthy is the undersized keyboard), but often is as powerful as a desktop.

null character

A data control character designed to take up time or space without altering operation in any other way.

null string

An empty string intended only to occupy space, such as to fill a *fixed length field* in a database where no hard data exists.

number

(1) Any of a set of symbols that represents a value achieved by counting.

(2) An element or position in a series.

number crunching

The manipulation of numeric data such as for the creation of financial reports and analyses with the use of a spreadsheet.

number keypad, numeric keypad

(1) A set of number keys similar to those on a calculator keyboard that is a part of most desktop computer keyboards.

(2) A small, special purpose keyboard, often connected to a laptop or notebook computer that lacks a number pad.

number system
(1) Any scheme for symbolizing values, such as decimal, hexidecimal, etc.
(2) A method of displaying values in which the position of an integer helps to determine its value.
In a decimal system, for example, $1=1$, $1n=10+n$, $1nn=100+nn$, etc.

numeral
A symbol that represents a number such as 1 through 9 in the decimal system, or 1 through 9 and A through F in a hexidecimal system.

numeric, numerical
Relating to a number or series of numbers.

numerical value See *absolute value*.

O

object
An element created in an application other than the one being run and that can be imported into it, such as a spreadsheet, graphic image, sound, or video, that can be attached to a word processing program. See also, *object linking and embedding*.

object linking and embedding *OLE*
The connecting of text, audio, video, or graphics data between documents and applications.

A *link* implies that changing the original allows automatic updating of the data in the host to which the object is linked.

An *embedded object* is one that is saved in a host file, but retains a connection with the application in which it was originally created so that the source application can be called up from within the host to edit the object.

The possibilities for OLE are endless:

- Linking large graphics or sound files keeps the host (or client) file to a manageable size. (And it saves disk space—an *imported* or *embedded* file is saved in two places, the *original file* and the *copy* saved in the document where it is being used.

- Linking allows the use of the same data in several documents with the assurance that they are all up to date—each document derives its data from the same source file which is the only place changes are made.

- Linking offers the opportunity to create sophisticated documents in which textual data or graphic images can be supplemented by sound or video images with the click of a mouse button.

- Embedding provides a means to edit material imported from a foreign format without exiting from the working document—a real plus when tailoring a spreadsheet, chart, or graphic image to a particular document, especially when there is no desire to change the original.

OCR See *optical character recognition.*

OCR program

A computer program that is intended to translate graphic images of letters and numbers to character bits that can manipulated by a word processor, spreadsheet, or other similar program.

The quality of such programs varies greatly—some programs require near–perfect conditions to achieve an acceptable **hit ratio** while others are able to sort out **background noise** and compensate for copy that is scanned in at an angle or that contains broken letters caused by poor copy or a bad scan. The most sophisticated programs are capable of 'learning' by recording corrections made by the user and compensating on future reads.

See also, *adaptive system*.

OCR reader See *scanner*.

octal

(1) Based on the number eight.

(2) A numbering system in base eight.

OEM *Original Equipment Manufacturer*

The manufacturer, as contrasted to a distributor or seller, of computer hardware.

office automation

The use of computers to accomplish tasks associated with running a business such as for recording sales, payroll, or accounts payable; writing checks; and controlling inventory records.

off line

(1) Descriptive of equipment that is not directly connected to or controlled by a central computer or computer network.

(2) An operation that is allied to, but separated from, another such as a cost accounting or payroll system that is independent of the main accounting program and provides data that is later fed into it.

(3) Equipment that is turned off.

OLE See *Object Linking and Embedding*.

one dimensional array See *array*.

on line

(1) A reference to equipment that is directly connected to or controlled by a central computer or computer network.

(2) A program or operation that is allied to another such as an inventory control program that is linked directly to accounts payable (goods purchased) and accounts receivable (goods sold) programs.

(3) Computer equipment that is turned on and connected to a controller.

on–line documentation

(1) Information that is displayed on a computer monitor screen as data is processed, such as the names of files being copied or moved to a new destination.

(2) Information that is available to a user from within a program such as a *help screen*.

on–line system

A computer system in which data from an input device is fed directly into a main computer and processed immediately or at regular intervals. A *bar code* scanner, for example, that records a sale at a store's cash register may also be connected to the store's computer in order to update inventory and sales reports.

on–screen controls

Descriptive of a peripheral such as a printer, monitor, scanner, or sound system that provides for adjusting settings from a panel on the computer screen. The advantage of on–screen controls is that they eliminated the manipulation of buttons or switches on or inside the hardware case, and the effects of the change(s) are is usually immediately apparent.

op code *operation code*

A symbol or set of symbols that direct the computer

133

open

to execute a command.

open

A file that has been copied from memory storage to RAM and is available for manipulation by the user.

open loop

A computer programming technique in which a *loop* is designed to pause after each repetition to request input from the user such as a *search* routine that displays the results of the search and requires the user to exit the routine or to provide instructions for another search.

operating manual

A book of instructions for the use of a particular application. Increasingly, operating manuals are shrinking as *help* files and *context sensitive help* become more detailed.

operating system

A program that directs all of the basic functions of a computer such as accepting commands from a keyboard, displaying input on a monitor screen, and controlling disk drives and some peripheral devices.

operation code See *op code*.

operator

A symbol that represents a mathematical or logical function, such as + (plus), = (equals), and > (greater than), used in computer formulas.

optical character recognition

A system for identifying scanned text or symbols and translating them into meaningful data that can be manipulated. Some devices scan symbols such as *bar codes* to record sales, inventory adjustments, etc. Others 'read' hard copy or a computer file to translate a graphic image into characters that can be saved in a word processing program and manipulated by the user. Recognition is attained by comparing the scanned image with a set of matrixes held in memory.

optical disk See *laser disk*.

optical fiber
A fine, flexible, tranparent fiber of glass or plastic, used to transmit data.

optical reader See *scanner*.

optical scanner See *scanner*.

optimized code
Of a program or routine that is carefully written to attain maximum efficiency, that is, one that directs the computer perform a task at optimum speed and with the use of a minimum of memory.

options
Choices available to the user. Options available to the user vary widely from one program to another. They offer such choices as how a program is to be displayed on the monitor screen, how much processing time is to be allocated to background operations, and whether to periodically save active documents.

OR
A selective operator used in programming, such as for a spreadsheet or database formula. The formula would be used to select elements that meet at least one of two (or more, see *nest*) criteria such as to produce a list of a company's customers who purchased only certain product lines.

order
To arrange in sequence.

OS See *operating system*.

OS/2 *Operating System 2*

A proprietary program that controls all of the basic operations of the computer.

out of range message

An error message encountered when a numerical *search* request is higher or lower than any contained in the database, such as a request for record number 200 in a database that contains 150 records, or for an accounts payable record listing for July 1994 from an accounting program that was set up in October 1995.

output

(1) Any information transferred from one device to another in a computer system as from computer memory to a printer.

(2) Information that has been processed and delivered to the user, such as to the monitor screen.

output device

A peripheral unit that delivers information to the user, as a monitor screen, printer, or plotter.

output limited

Descriptive of processing speed or capacity that is hindered by the speed at which output can be achieved.

The most common limitation is printing—the computer can typically process data much faster than a printer can format and print it. Often there is nothing the user can do except wait for a document to be printed. Modern systems generally offer both hardware and software solutions: printers equipped with large amounts of memory and internal processors coupled with computer operating systems that permit printing as **background processing** both serve to free up the application for the user. Printing itself may not be any faster, but at least you don't have to wait for it!

overflow

(1) A condition occurring when the available data is greater than the space allocated to hold it, as in a fixed length database field. Overflow of a database field or any fixed field in a program can result in a loss of data or incorrect results when computations are based on the oversized entry.

(2) That portion of data which goes beyond the limits of the space allocated for displaying it. This overflow in a spreadsheet cell may be displayed by an asterisk or a dash; however, the complete information is likely retained in memory thus allowing correct calculations based on the data even though it can't be displayed on the screen.

overhead

(1) The amount of volatile memory that is used for various operating and utility functions, and is therefore not available for running a program.

(2) The storage space on a disk that is forfeited to formatting and **File Allocation Tables**.

overload

A condition that can cause a program to crash, brought on by an attempt to transfer more data than memory can hold or transferring data faster than the CPU can process it.

overwrite

To save information to a storage area that is already

occupied, thus obliterating the old data. Typically, when saving a file, we overwrite the old data, although there are exceptions—see ***nondistructive read***.

P

pack
(1) A database program command that erases database records marked for deletion.
(2) To ***defragment*** computer files.
(3) To compress computer data for more efficient operation and use of disk storage space.

packaged software
Any program adaptable to a variety of uses that is available on the open market. See also, ***bundled***.

packet
A block of computer data that is transmitted as a unit.

page
(1) A fixed quantity of memory used by a computer to facilitate the movement of data between permanent storage and RAM. See also, ***cluster***.
(2) A single sheet of data in a word processing program or delivered as output from a printer.

page addressing
A technique by which a computer manages a large amount of data by first separating it into smaller parts or pages (see ***page (1)***, above) which can be more easily manipulated.

page break
The point at which copy ends on a single page, set up either as a default for an entire document or file,

or as indicated by a special user command.

page heading See *header*.

page reader See *scanner*.

pagination
The numbering of printed pages in a document or file.

paint program
An application for creating artwork or graphics as for insertion into a document, spreadsheet, etc. A paint program customarily uses *bitmap* or *raster imaging* techniques.

paper feeder
A device that controls the flow of single sheets of paper or a continuous form through a printer.

parallel
(1) Descriptive of operations that occur simultaneously or side by side.
(2) Descriptive of a device that is controlled through the *parallel port* of a computer, such as a *parallel printer*.

parallel interface
A multichannel interface that allows the transfer of a full computer word at one time.

parallel port
A *parallel interface* connection on a computer for communicating with a peripheral device, such as a printer.

parameter
A limit, as of a particular program or computer operating system.

parse
To break down into discrete parts, as in separating

elements of a data string extracted from a database into columnar data for a spreadsheet.

partition

(1) A divider.

(2) The division of a large hard disk into smaller segments for more efficient management of programs and data.

When the *physical drive* or disk is segmented into more than one *logical drive*, the first partition is referred to as the *primary partition* and the remainder of the logical drives as *extended partitions*. Dividing a large physical drive into smaller partitions provides:

• Smaller *clusters* and less wasted space on a disk;

• Easier incremental backups when, for example, programs are on one logical drive and data is on another; and

• Less *seek time* for data (although tests have shown that there is little effect on overall performance).

On the down side, partitioning a disk can be limiting. There may not be enough space within a logical drive to install a new program or upgrade, or to accommodate a set of large graphics or multimedia files. The sum of the leftover, unusable space in the logical drives may be more than would be sacrificed to larger clusters if the drive were not partitioned.

(3) The segmenting of records for more efficient processing of a database sort.

passive

Descriptive of an *LCD* computer screen that uses a *multiplexer* to refresh the pixels that make up the screen image. Passive imaging refreshes one row or pixels at a time, so pixels tend to fade before the next reflex thus causing a flicker. A *single–scan* screen is less expensive than an **active matrix** and causes less drain on the battery power of a portable, but suffers from poor image quality. A *dual–scan* screen has two multiplexers, each serving half the screen and thus provides a faster screen refresh rate and improved image over single–scan.

password
A series of characters or symbols by which a user gains access to a computer, application, or file, and that is intended to prevent access by unauthorized users.

path
(1) The logical or designated route followed by a computer in seeking commands, programs, and data files from within a **hierarchical** file structure.
(2) An opertating system command that specifies the location of specific programs or data.

pattern recognition
The technique used by a program to identify elements through comparison with a standard matrix as in **optical character recognition**.

PC
(1) *Personal Computer* A microcomputer designed for individual use at home or in a business. Generally, a **desktop computer**, **laptop computer**, or **notebook computer**.
(2) *Printed Circuit* An electronic circuit in which the connecting elements are printed or imbedded on an insulated base.

PC card See *PCMCIA card*.

PCI

PCI *Peripheral Component Interface*
An advanced 32– and 64–bit bus created by Intel.

PCL *Printer Control Language*
A common protocol for laser printers used by Hewlett–Packard and printers compatible with H–P. See also, *PostScript*.

PCMCIA *Personal Computer Memory Card International Association*
A trade association formed in 1989 to formulate specifications for removable memory cards, their slots, and their software interface.

PCMCIA card, PC card

A memory card approximately the size of a bank credit card, but somewhat thicker, that connects to a slot on a PC to add such things as programs, hard drive type storage, a fax/modem, or a **SCSI** port. The small size, durability, and *plug–and–play* capabilities of PCMCIA cards makes them a natural for portable PC's.

Although all PCMCIA cards use the same type of connectors and are the same size (length and width), there are basically three types, each of a different thickness. A slot configured for the thickest (Type III) will accommodate the thinner cards, but obviously the reverse is not true. Implementation of the standard may also vary from one manufacturer to another. In short, the buyer of a PCMCIA card needs to make certain that the card will fit the computer's slot and work with its system.

.PCX *PC Paintbrush*
A file name extension for a bitmapped image, a type of graphics file.

PDA *Personal Digital Assistant*
Any of a number of small (from 3" by 5" to 5" by 7" and about 1" thick) communication devices that go by such names as *MessagePad, Magic Link, Omnigo,* or *Zaurus.* Features vary from one machine to another, but they sport quite a variety for such a small package: an electronic note pad that records input from a small keyboard or from characters written on the screen with a stylus, an address book, appointment calendar, calculator, or spreadsheet. They send and retrieve ***E-mail*** and faxes, connect to online services, and transfer data to a personal computer or another PDA via modem.

peer-to-peer network
A scheme in which networked computers share resources; each workstation may be either ***client*** or ***server***. See also, ***dedicated network***.

peripheral, peripheral device
Non-essential equipment that is connected to a computer and controlled by it such as a printer or scanner.

peripheral program, peripheral software
(1) A utility; a program that adds to the capabilities of a computer or a program run on the computer, such as a memory manager or grammar checker.
(2) A program that manages a peripheral device.

permanent memory
A storage medium, such as a computer hard disk, that retains its memory when power is turned off.

personal information manager See ***PIM***.

phosphor
The coating on the inside of a ***CRT*** that emits a

.PIC

burst of light when struck by electron particles.

.PIC *Picture*

A file name extension for a Lotus vector image, a type of graphics file.

picture

A graphic element, especially one imported from an external source. See also *object*.

PIM *Personal Information Manager*

A utility program that provides a means to record, organize, and retrieve data important to an individual, such as random notes, appointments, or addresses.

pincushioning

A computer monitor screen distortion characterized by an image that is full width at the top and bottom of the screen, but bowed in or compressed across the center.

pin feed

A device that feeds a continuous form through a printer by engaging a series of holes along the edges of the form; same as *tractor feed* or *sprocket feed*.

pirated software

A computer program obtained outside normal or legal channels.

pitch

The density, or number of characters per inch of a type font.

pixel *Picture Element*

The basic, smallest component of a computer screen image and certain graphic representations, such as a *bitmap*.

place marker See *bookmark*.

platen
The roller that paper rests against while images are being formed by an impact printer.

platform
An operating system such as MS–DOS® or OS/2®, or a graphics interface such as Windows® under which a program runs.

plotter
A computer peripheral that produces charts or graphs as output.

plug–and–play
(1) The capability of an operating system to identify a new peripheral when it is installed, and to communicate without special configuring by the operator.
(2) The quality of **PCMCIA** technology that allows changing cards without shutting down the computer.

point of sale system
A computer network that accepts input from remote terminals located at a retailer's cash register and uses the data to perform a variety of tasks such as creating sales reports, updating inventory records, etc.

point and click
The technique for selecting an object by moving the mouse cursor to it, then pressing and releasing the mouse button.

Polish notation
A system of expressing algebraic or arithmetic formulas in which parentheses are not used and the operator (such as + or -) precedes the number on which the operation is to be performed.

polling
An I/O function that scans transmission lines to
check their status and ascertain when data is to be
sent or received.

port
Any of the connections to a computer that allow the
transfer of data.

portable hard disk
A *hard disk* and its drive that are connected to a
computer although not mounted in the cabinet, and
that can be removed and attached to another computer that is set up with the proper connections and
software.

portability
(1) Descriptive of the relative ease with which data
can be transferred between certain programs.
(2) A measure of the size and weight of a computer
or peripherals that make them easily transportable.

PostScript®
The page description language used by *Aldus©*,
originally for the *MacIntosh®* computer. *PostScript®*
is designed to be more precise with graphics than
PCL although the gap has narrowed considerably.
Most service bureaus conform to the *PostScript®*
standard.

power management
A technique for conserving power, especially in a
battery–operated device, such as for powering down
the monitor screen in the absence of foreground activity.

power supply
A device that converts AC power to low level DC

power for a computer.

power surge

A sudden increase in line voltage that can damage computer hardware and software.

power up

To turn on a piece of equipment.

precedence

(1) The order in which arithmetic operations in an algebraic formula are processed by the computer. Establishing such precedence can be critical to the results obtained from a database or spreadsheet formula. For example,

n_1+n_2/n_3 [n_1 added to the result of dividing n_2 by n_3]

will yield a different result than:

$(n_1+n_2)/n_3$ [n_1 added to n_2 and the sum divided by n_3].

(2) The ordering of processing, as by selecting which type of processing has priority over another.

preprocessing

The configuration of data before it is entered into a program, such as converting spreadsheet data to comma separated values for entering into the fields of a database.

primary DOS partition See *partition*.

print control character

Any of the symbols or combinations of symbols that control the operation or output of the printer, as for line spacing, line feed, form feed, double width characters, etc.

Printer Control Language See *PCL*.

printed circuit

A circuit created by applying a conductor to an insulated base.

printer font
(1) A type font programmed into a printer or supplied through a cartridge attached to a printer. (2) Program instructions sent to a printer to allow it to format specific output in order to more quickly free up the CPU. See also, *screen font*.

printer port
The connection on a computer or terminal that provides a link to a printer.

print positions
The number of fixed spaced font characters that can be printed on a line of a specific length.

Print Screen (key)
A function key that commands the computer to copy data on the monitor screen to the printer.

processing
The manipulation of data by a computer.

processor
A *CPU*; the integrated circuits that control the operation of a microcomputer.

production control program
A system for allocating materials and scheduling the people and processes associated with a manufacturing operation.

program
A set of directions that instruct the computer in the performance of a task.

program compatibility
Descriptive of the ability of programs to work together or to share data.

programmable
Descriptive of an application or device the function

of which can be altered or manipulated by the user.

programmable function key

A function key to which a command or series of commands can be assigned.

programmable buttons, programmable mouse

Descriptive of a mouse or mouse buttons (other than the main button) that may be assigned a command or series of commands, often in conjunction with key combinations. For example, pressing a second or third button to execute a *double click*, pressing a button in conjunction with a Shift, Ctrl, or Alt key or a combination of them to activate a frequently used program, utility, or routine.

programmer

An individual who creates or alters routines for a computer.

programming language

(1) A precise system of vocabulary and syntax for writing instructions for the computer.

(2) A high level language.

program package

(1) All of the computer files and instruction manuals needed to run a program.

(2) Descriptive of the qualities and capabilities that make up a program.

(3) A set of applications, as for various accounting functions, that make up a complete program.

prompt

(1) A cursor; a highlight on the computer screen that indicates where the next character or instruction will be entered.

(2) A pop-up query or instruction for the user that is

proportional spacing

activated by a program or routine when certain conditions are met.

proportional spacing

Descriptive of the display of type so that the amount of white space between characters is approximately the same regardless of the width of the character itself. See also, *fixed spacing*.

proprietary software

Packaged software that is sold with the understanding that the seller retains ownership and the buyer purchases only the right to use the software subject to the provisions of a licensing agreement.

protected field

(1) A block of text, formula, etc. that cannot be altered. Spreadsheet cells that contain formulas, for example, may be protected by the user so as to prevent inadvertently overwriting them.

(2) A portion of a monitor screen that cannot be changed with the keyboard, mouse, or other input device, such as the field name in a database record.

protected files

(1) Read–only files; computer memory that may be read, but that cannot be altered.

(2) Files that are safeguarded by a password so that they are not available to an unauthorized user.

protocol

The rules governing the transfer of data within a computer, between a computer and peripherals, or between computers.

public domain software

Programs that are not copyrighted and that may be used or altered by anyone.

Q

QBE *Query By Example*
A feature of some database programs that allows the operator to fill in part of a blank record or data entry screen, then search for all matching records. For example, by filling in "Brown" in a LASTNAME field and "32301" in a ZIPCODE field, the search engine will bring up all the records for persons named *Brown* who live in area code *32301*.

QIC *Quarter–Inch Cartridge*
A type of tape cartridge or drive for backing up computer data that uses a tape .25" wide.

quad–speed
Descriptive of a compact disk drive or other device that retrieves data or operates at roughly four times the speed of earlier standard units.

qualifier
A symbol or set of symbols in a formula that limits or more clearly defines an element such as of a database search for persons residing in a specific zip code area.

query
A request for data, as a record or set of records from a database.

query language
The formal notation for requesting specific data, as from a database.

query by example
A database search technique that allows the user to search for records by entering a value or instruction in a data entry form.

queue
A list of elements that are ready for processing and that will be acted on as resources become available, such as files or documents ready to be printed, or fax messages that are ready to be sent.

quick swap See *hot swap*.

QWERTY keyboard
A keyboard with letters arranged in the same order as those on a typewriter. QWERTY are the first six letters in the upper tier of keys. See also *DSK Dvorak Simplified Keyboard*.

R

ragged right
Descriptive of lines of type that are formatted to line up with the left margin of a document, but not the right margin.

RAM *Random Access Memory*
Fast, volatile memory that may be accessed independent of the previous call. RAM is used in the computer to store programs and data that are being accessed by the user. Also called *main memory*, RAM is erased when power is shut down. Many printers, especially laser printers, are equipped with additional RAM to allow storage and formatting of pages queued for printing so as to free up the computer more quickly.

RAM cache
Memory used to store data that is often called into use. On a video card, for example, the *RAM cache* may hold the contents of windows that are hidden from view in order to provide rapid screen refresh

when the window is brought into view.

RAMDAC *Random Access Memory Digital To Analog Converter*

A chip that converts digital data from the computer to analog data used by certain other devices, such as a monitor screen.

range

(1) The extent or scope of a variable.

(2) A user–defined limit of records that are to be selected from a database, for example a list of transactions that took place before or after a certain date, or between two dates; a list of transactions with a particular client or vendor; or a list of sales over a certain amount.

(3) The portion of a spread sheet file that is to be printed, defined by specifying the location of the first cell and the last cell in the range.

(4) A set of spreadsheet cells similarly identified that are to be acted on by a command, often a *named range* (see ***name***).

raster image

A type of graphic image commonly produced by a ***paint program***. The image is a ***bitmap*** composed of ***pixels*** that suffer a loss of resolution when scaled and that may be more difficult to manipulate within a program than a ***vector image*** that is constructed in layers.

read

(1) To access information from computer storage.

(2) To input information as by a ***scanner***.

read error

A system interrupt that is triggered when the

computer is unable to access a particular area of
data. Read errors are commonly caused by a simple
malfunction of the computer or by damage to the
disk or other medium on which the data is stored.
Generally, a computer malfunction can be resolved
by exiting the operation or program, then trying
again. Damage to the storage medium is more serious, but there are utility programs that can assist in
recovering all or most of the data.

read–only
Descriptive of a computer file that may be accessed,
but not altered. See also, *file attribute*.

read/write head
The device in a disk drive that reads from and writes
to the storage disk.

real time, real time processing
(1) The period required for the computer to complete
a specific task, from the time of the entry of data or
the issuance of a command until processing is completed.
(2) Descriptive of *foreground* processing as it occurs, especially that which requires periodic input
from the user that is immediately acted on by the
computer.

record
The group of fields that make up a unique entry in a
database.

record format
The configuration and arrangement of fields in a
database record. See also, *field format*.

recording head
That part of a disk drive that writes data for

permanent storage on a disk or other medium.

record length

In a fixed length database, the number of spaces or characters required to accommodate all of the fields in a record.

reformat

(1) To change the style of text in a document.

(2) To convert a computer file for use by a different application.

refresh

(1) To revive or renew volatile memory such as *RAM* so as to retain or alter it.

(2) To repeatedly redraw the image on the monitor screen so as to make the image appear stable.

refresh rate

The number of times per second a computer screen is refreshed or updated, expressed in *hertz* (Hz). Commonly, monitors have a refresh rate of 60 Hz, although rates up to 72 Hz are available and much easier on the eyes, even if the difference in the screen image isn't immediately apparent.

register

(1) A part of the CPU where data is held during processing.

(2) To record the purchase of hardware or software with the vendor so as to exercise one's right to technical support, warrantee coverage, etc.

relational database

A database that contains information associated with that in one or more different databases and that has a field in common with the others so that information may be drawn from some or all and

relational operator

combined to create a new database, report, etc. See also, *database set*.

relational operator

A mathematical symbol that represents the relationship between two values such as = (equal to) or > (greater than).

relative address, relative addressing

An *address* or location for data held in computer storage that is calculated from the location of a previous call. For example, in a *fixed length field* database, individual fields and records may not have *absolute addresses*; succeeding fields in a record or succeeding records in the database are located by calculating their location in relation to the field or record being accessed.

REM *REMark*

A program command that instructs the computer to ignore the rest of the line and that is used to place a comment or explanatory note in a program without concern that the computer will view it as a command. The means for designating a comment line does vary depending on the particular programming language however.

remote

(1) Descriptive of a computer or peripheral that is not in the immediate area of the host computer.

(2) Descriptive of communications between computers over telephone lines.

remote access

The ability of a computer to connect and interact with another computer or peripheral that is not in the immediate area.

remote entry system
(1) A data entry terminal that is located at a distance from the host computer, such as *shop floor collection* in a manufacturing operation, or sales information from the checkout stations in a large store.
(2) Hardware or software that permits access to a base computer from another connected to a telephone line.

removable storage
Any of a number of devices for storing data that are transportable outside the computer such as:
• CD's
• floppy disks
• removable hard disks
• tapes

repeat key
A program feature that provides for the use of a function key or key combination to repeat the last entry from the keyboard, such as a line of typing or a formatting command.

report
A document in the computer or that is output to a hard copy that summarizes the outcome from data processing.

report format
(1) The configuration of a report as for heading, page numbers, fonts, etc. output from a database or spreadsheet file.
(2) A saved file of user–defined specifications for a particular report.

reserved word, reserved symbol
A word or symbol that has a special meaning in a

reset

particular programming language.

reset

(1) To command a return to a previous or ready condition, such as to wipe special formatting data from a printer's memory after a print job is completed.

(2) To restart the computer.

resolution

The relative fineness of the image on a computer screen or that produced by a printer or scanner. Resolution is usually expressed as *dpi*, or dots per inch for a scanner or printer, and in *pixels* for the image on a computer monitor screen.

resources

The sum of all the capabilities of a computer system determined by its hardware and software configuration.

restore

To return to a previous condition, as a program feature that deletes the effect of the last entry from the keyboard, such as by typing or formatting.

RET *Resolution Enhancement Technology*

A technique developed by Hewlett–Packard® to smooth the rough edges of a printed image and improve its *resolution*.

Return (key) Same as *Enter* key.

reverse video

The display on a computer monitor screen of dark characters on a light background.

right justified

Of type that is aligned along the right margin of a document and is more or less ragged on the left.

ring

A computer network configuration in which the workstations are connected in a circle.

ROM *Read–Only Memory*

Memory such as that built into the operating system of a computer that can be accessed, but that cannot be altered.

root directory

The primary directory in a hierarchical file structure that holds the first tier of named directories as well as the operating system command and system configuration files.

rotate

A program feature that provides for the decorative turning or tilting of text or graphics in a document.

routine

A group of computer commands designed to perform a particular task.

row

The horizontal arrangement of data in a two or three dimensional array.

run time

The period required for a computer to perform a particular task, such as a mail merge.

S

.SAM

File name extension for a particular type of *word processor* file.

save

A program command that writes data to non–volitile memory.

scalable font

Descriptive of a *typeface* that can be reproduced accurately in a wide range of sizes in contrast to a *bitmap font* that requires a separate image file for each point size.

Scalable fonts make use of mathematical formulas to produce an outline or matrix of each character in the font. In its simplest configuration, changing point size involves merely scaling the formula up or down. In some cases, such as for unusually large fonts, it also involves altering proportions so as to present a more pleasing visual image.

scanner

An optical device for reading hard copy and translating it to digital data. Data read by a scanner is captured as a *graphic element* that can be minipulated by a paint or draw program, but not by a word processing program unless it is converted into alphanumeric characters.

See also, *optical character recognition.*

screen

The device that displays information as it is entered as from a keyboard or scanner, reports on processing by the computer, and that generally monitors its activity.

screen blanker

A utility program that prevents burning an image into a computer monitor screen by blacking out the screen after a specified period of inactivity. A type of *screen saver.*

screen refresh

The constant renewal of the image on a computer

monitor screen in order to provide the appearance of a steady image.

screen font
A font set generated to create a computer screen image that closely emulates the look of the font when it is printed.

screen form
A questionnaire or other document displayed on a computer monitor screen that allows information to be entered in the appropriate places and that can be saved to a computer file.

screen refresh
The repeated redrawing of the image on a monitor screen so as to maintain it and make the image appear stable.

screen saver
A utility that blanks a computer screen or that displays a random moving pattern on the screen after a user–defined period of inactivity.

scrolling
The shifting of the image on a computer screen to allow viewing of elements outside the screen's borders.

SCSI *Small Computer System Interface*
A controller that transfers data at high speeds and supports multiple peripherals through a single PC expansion slot

search
A feature in some programs that locates a word or phrase in text files, records in a database file, or a particular file.

search and replace See *global search and replace*.

search object
An element, as a name or symbol, that is the basis for a search command.

sector
One of the segments into which a computer disk data *track* is divided, 512 bytes; the smallest unit of data addressed by the disk controller.

security See *computer security*.

seek time
The average time it takes to position a hard disk read/write head over data being sought.

select
To choose from the alternatives offered.

select word See *reserved word*.

sequential
Ordered; descriptive of data, files, etc. arranged or accessed in a particular order.

sequential search
An orderly progression through data, files, etc., one after another, until the object of the search is found.

serial interface
A connector that transmits data sequentially, one bit a time over a single line. A serial interface is considerably slower than a *parallel interface* that transmit a full computer word, or eight bits, simultaneously.

serial port
A connection on a computer for communicating with a peripheral device.

server
A computer whose resources such as storage and printer are available to other terminals in a

computer network known as **clients**. In a **dedicated network**, the server is not a workstation. In a **peer-to-peer network**, any or all terminals may be client *and* server.

shared resources

Descriptive of devices, peripherals, programs, etc. that serve two or more computers or terminals.

shareware

Software that can be downloaded from the Internet, an on-line service, bulletin board, etc. or ordered from a shareware distributor. The software is available without charge—shareware distributors charge for the disks only—for a trial run by the user. Registration with the developer and payment for continued use is on the honor system. Most developers offer an upgrade or additional applications when the programs is registered.

sheet feeder

(1) A device that can be filled with a number of sheets of paper or other carrier to automatically load into the printer. The sheet feeder may be an integral part of the printer or purchased as an attachment. See also **envelope feeder**, **tractor feed**.

(2) An attachment that allows the continuous feeding of multiple sheets of copy into a scanner.

shielded

Descriptive of cable that is insulated to prohibit the transfer of signals to or from another line.

shift

(1) To change position or function.

(2) A type of special key—Shift, Ctrl, Alt—that alone or in combination with other keys are used to

shop floor collection

execute commands. See also, *function key*.

shop floor collection

The collection of data from workers in a factory. Shop floor collection may be simply an electronic time clock which records starting and quiting time for each employee, or it may involve stations throughout the plant where employees record their beginning and ending time of work on a particular job or process.

shortcut key

A combination of a character or function key with a shift key, used to execute a command or *macro*.

shovelware

Descriptive of software that is of little or no value, often utilities or reference material, offered in addition to a program to increase the perceived value of the package.

simulation

A representation or imitation, especially with the help of a computer, such as for instruction (flight simulation) or entertainment (*virtual reality*).

simultaneous processing

The processing by a computer of two or more tasks at the same time.

single–scan See *passive*.

single–user

(1) Descriptive of software that is licensed for use by one person only. Applications that are to be accessed by several users, as on a network, usually carry a higher licensing fee.

(2) Descriptive of a computer system that provides for input by a single user only. See also, *network*.

slack space See *cluster*.

slave

(1) Any device that is controlled by input from a computer.

(2) A computer that serves only as a *server* in a *dedicated network*.

slot

An opening in a computer frame designed to plug in an add-on card. Most computers are equipped wth several open slots to allow for the later addition of devices that are not part of the original equipment such as an advanced video controller, sound card, CD player, etc.

slow storage

Any memory device, usually external, that is slow in the accessing or transferring of data relative to the speed of a hard disk drive. Such a device is usually used to store seldom used data or to back up a computer during down time.

smart card

(1) A credit card or similar device that contains a *magnetic strip* for the retention of data.

(2) A *PCMCIA card*.

snail mail

A derisive term used by *E-mail* subscribers to describe the postal service.

soft carriage return

In some word processing programs, a forced end to a line of text within a paragraph.

Unlike the manual or electric typewriter that requires the user to enter a carriage return at the end of each line, most computer word processing programs provide for word wrapping, a feature that enables text to overflow to the next line automatically. Pressing the *Enter* key in the computer program signals the beginning of a new paragraph. The soft carriage return in the computer program allows one to override the word wrap feature and emulate the typewriter carriage return by breaking a line at the position of the user's choosing.

soft hyphen

An embedded hyphen that appears between syllables of a word only when the word is broken at the end of a line of text.

software

Any program or routine, such as an application, system file, device driver, etc. that furnishes instructions to the computer.

software documentation

Instructions for the loading and operation of a software program.

software font

(1) A downloadable font; a **bitmap font** that must be downloaded to a printer. A bitmap font is somewhat less convenient to use than a **font cartridge** or a **scalable font** because it requires downloading in the sizes and styles that are contained in a particular document prior to printing. Further, the number of fonts that can be used in a document is limited by the printer memory available to hold them.

(2) A *scalable font* is also created from software, but is not so much a font as a program that creates fonts in a variety of sizes and styles; therefore, the term *software font* generally is used in reference to

the older bitmap fonts.

software utility

Any program that assists in the operation of the computer or of another program as by enhancing or improving performance, managing files, etc.

sort

To place data or files in a predetermined order, as alphabetical, by number, by date, by size, etc.

sort field, sort key

The field in a database file or column of a spreadsheet file on which a sort is based such as by last name, date of birth, or zip code.

sound card

An add–on card that drives a sound system and provides a connector for external speakers, microphone input, etc.

sound driver

The program that controls the recording, manipulation, and reproduction of sound in a multimedia computer.

sound file

Sound saved as digital data in a computer file.

source data

(1) Data that has been entered into a computer for manipulation.

(2) The source documents that provide verification of data entered into a computer such as for providing a part of the audit trail in an accounting program.

space

(1) A computer interval that is not occupied by a character, a zero, or a blank.

(2) An unprinted character on a computer monitor

screen or printed page.

special character
(1) Any printed character that is not a letter or a number, such as a punctuation mark or a mathematical symbol.
(2) An unprinted command character such as a paragraph mark or non breaking space.

speech recognition
(1) The techniques and equipment that permit control of a computer with vocal commands.
(2) Of the ability of a computer to accept and act on voice commands.

speech synthesis
The emulation of human speech by a computer through the use of recorded sounds or construction from digital data.

speed key
A character or function key used in combination with a shift key to execute a command.

spell checker
A feature in a word processor program, or a separate utility, that checks and corrects spelling in a document.

spike
(1) A momentary sharp increase in electrical current that may damage a computer or its memory.
(2) A program feature that permits a number of independent elements to be removed from a document to a buffer from which they can be inserted elsewhere as a unit.

split screen
A program or operating system feature that permits

viewing two different files or different parts of a single file at the same time and manipulating them independently.

spooler
A hardware or software device that can be used to store computer output so that it can be piped to the printer in sequential order with little or no disturbance to foreground processing, or to be printed at a later time.

spreadsheet
A document with data arranged in rows and columns that can be adjusted for the entry of additional data and manipulated for reporting.

spreadsheet cell
A basic data unit in a spreadsheet.

spreadsheet formula
A command or equation placed in a spreadsheet cell that produces the result of the manipulation of other data in the spreadsheet, such as for determining a total of the values in a group of cells.

sprocket feed
A printer device that feeds a continuous form through the printer by engaging a series of holes along the edges of the form; same as *pin feed* or *tractor feed*.

SQL *Structured Query Language*
A type of computer standard for retrieving database records from a remote database.

stack
An area of memory in RAM reserved for the temporary storage of data, 'stacked' in the order it was last called. This stacking technique, designed to improve

standard interface

computer preformance, is based on the theory that the items called most recently are among those most likely to be called again soon.

standard interface

Any hardware or software connection between a computer and a peripheral that complies with an industry standard.

star

A computer network configuration in which the workstations are connected to a common *hub* or *concentrator*.

static memory

Computer memory that is retained when the power is off, such as the *ROM* that drives the computer or that memory on a *hard disk*, *floppy disk*, *CD*, tape, etc. where programs and data are stored.

statistical analysis

The evaluation of a body of numerical data relating to a particular subject.

step

Any one of a series of related actions.

storage

The area of non–volatile memory in a computer such as on a hard disk or an external device, as a diskette or tape, where copies of program and data files are kept for future use.

storage capacity

The volume of data, expressed in bytes, that can be contained in a storage device.

string

A series of characters or symbols processed as a unit.

structured programming
Any of a number of systems for organizing and writing a computer program so as to reduce the chance for misinterpretation or error.

structured query language See *SQL*.

stylesheet
A formatting template that can be created in some programs to establish a master document page with such basic specifications as page margins, indents, type fonts and styles, etc. for certain types of documents or spreadsheets.

subscript
In typesetting, a character that is positioned below the baseline of the body of text, as H_2SO_4

suffix
An addendum to a computer file name, separated from the name by a period, that aids in identifying the file contents, as *.SYS* for a system file, *.TXT* for a text file, etc.

summarize
(1) To abbreviate by discarding unnecessary detail.
(2) To condense data by totaling like elements.

superscript
In typesetting, a character that is positioned above the baseline of the body of text, as x^2.

super VGA
An advanced, *VESA*-created video graphics display mode standard used to drive a variety of color and resolution combinations for a computer monitor screen.

support services
Ongoing help available to the user from hardware or

surge

software manufacturers or vendors, often via a toll–free hot line or bulletin board.

surge
A sudden increase in electrical current that may damage a computer or its memory

surge suppresser
A device that is designed to protect the computer and peripherals from power surges.

SVGA See *super VGA*.

swap file
A dedicated section of a hard drive or network drive used to trade information with *main memory*. The swap file is *virtual memory*—hard disk storage that can be used to emulate *RAM*—and is employed to temporarily hold data when RAM is full. This allows calling up more programs and data at one time than would normally be allowed by using RAM alone.

symbol
(1) Any of the characters available from the computer keyboard.
(2) A defined element within a program such as a mark or word that represents a command or instruction.

symbolic language
Any computer programming language that must be translated into machine language in order to run; a high level language.

symbolic logic
The use of symbols in a formula to test the relationship between elements.

symbolic name
A label that identifies a program, a file, a data field,

172

a range of data, etc.

syntax

The rules governing the precise way that statements must be constructed in a programming language.

synthesizer

An electronic musical instrument that can be used to record music to a computer file.

.SYS

File name extension for a system file, one that specifies device drivers, operating parameters, etc. for a computer or program.

system

An orderly arrangement of related elements, as all of the hardware devices that make up a *computer system* or all of the hardware, software, and procedures that make up an *accounting system*.

system backup

(1) A reserved copy of all of the program and data files in a computer.

(2) A second set of hardware and software that can replace the primary system in the event of equipment failure.

system board A *motherboard*.

system disk

A disk that contains the basic configuration and command files of an operating system required by a computer, commonly referring to a floppy disk that contains the operating system files.

system prompt

The symbols or characters on a computer screen that indicate the **command line** where instructions to the operating system are normally entered.

system resources
All of the elements unique to a particular computer system, as peripheral devices, type of CPU, memory, etc.

system software
The programs that control the operation of a computer and all of its peripherals.

T

tab
(1) Tabulator; a user–defined position on a text line to which the cursor can be advanced with a single key stroke.
(2) To move by activating the *tab key*.

tab key
A cursor control key that moves the insertion point according to program instructions, such as to a fixed position on a line of text, to the adjacent cell in a spreadsheet, or to the next item on a menu.

table
An orderly arrangement of related data in rows and columns; a two dimensional array.

table lookup
To locate a variable as a function of two values in a two dimensional array.

tape backup
A reserve copy of computer programs and data stored on magnetic tape.

target
An objective, as a file or device to which data is to be transmitted, or a directory to which a file is to be copied or saved.

task
A job assigned to the computer.

TCP/IP *Transmission Control Protocol/Internet Protocol*
The standard procedure for regulating transmission on the Internet.

technical support
Help available to a hardware or software user by the manufacturer, often via a toll free telephone line or a bulletin board.

temporary storage
The computer's main memory, the area that holds program and data files that are active.

terminal
Any device connected to a main computer or *file server* for the purpose of entering data or monitoring activity. The terminal usually consists of an input device such as a keyboard and a monitor screen. A *desktop computer* or *diskless workstation* most commonly serve as terminals in a network.

test
To subject hardware or software to diagnostics or sample problems in order to ascertain that a device or program is working properly.

test data
Data whose output is known for a particular formula or routine and is used to verify correct operation.

test run
To operate with test data to confirm the validity of a formula or routine.

text
(1) The body of a document.
(2) Any combination of characters and symbols that

conveys a message.

text editor

A basic program used to create or alter text without special formatting.

three dimensional array

An ordered group of like elements, aligned in rows, columns and layers.

three dimensional graphics

The simulation on a computer screen of a three dimensional object.

.TIF *TIFF, Tagged Image File Format*

A file name extension for a bitmapped image, a type of graphics file.

toggle

(1) A switch that may be set to either of two stable states.

(2) To select one of two options or states.

topology

The physical or logical configuration of a computer network.

touch terminal

A type of computer screen that permits the selection of options or the entry of data by touching areas of the screen.

track

One of the concentric circles of data on a computer disk. See also, *sector*.

trackball

A device, similar in function to a mouse, but with a fixed base holding a sphere that is manipulated to move the cursor. Some trackballs are mounted on or near the keyboard, especially in laptop or notebook computers.

tracking

The movement of a mouse pointer or other device on a computer monitor display screen.

tractor feed

A device that feeds a continuous form through a printer by engaging a series of holes along the edges of the form; same as *pin feed* or *sprocket feed.*

transaction

A completed action.

transaction file

A record of recent transactions used to update a master file such as a recording of daily sales used to update the sales account, receivables, cash account, inventory, etc.

transaction terminal

A device that permits remote input of data directly to the computer, such as on a shop floor or at a cash register.

transfer

To move data or files from one location, storage device or computer to another.

transform

To change the form of data without altering its significance or value, as from a group of database fields to a set of spreadsheet columns.

transient

Temporary, as a file that is created by a program while it is in use, then deleted when processing is completed.

transient voltage

A fluctuation in standard voltage, such as caused by

translate

a *brownout* or *spike* that can damage a computer or its data.

translate

(1) To change signals to a different format, as from analog to digital.

(2) To adapt data files to a format that can be read by a different program.

transmission

The transfer of signals between parts of a computer system.

transmission speed

The rate at which data can be sent and received, usually expressed as a *baud rate*.

transparent

Descriptive of computer processing that is taking place in the background, not under the direct supervision of, or apparent to, the user.

trapezoidal distortion

Distortion of the image on a computer screen characterized by sides of the image that are not parallel, or out of square.

tree

A graphic representation of a hierarchical directory structure showing the directories that branch from the root directory, then their subdirectories, etc.

troubleshoot

To attempt to locate the source of a hardware or software problem and correct it.

truncate

To shorten by eliminating less significant parts, as by rounding a decimal number or eliminating leading zeros in a number.

TSR *Terminate and Stay Resident*
A program feature, such as a pop–up note pad, that remains stored in RAM when not in use, available to be called up in the active window as needed.

tutorial
An adjunct to a program that describes its features and teaches the user how to use the program.

TWAIN
The standard protocol for scanning images.

two dimensional array
An ordered group of like elements, formed in rows and columns.

.TXT
File name extension for a text file.

type ahead buffer
An area of memory that stores key strokes that are entered faster than they can be processed.

typeface
A set of type of a particular design, as *Bodoni*, *Garamond*, etc.

type font See *font*.

type style
A particular style of a typeface, as *bold*, *italic*, *demi-bold*, etc.

U

UART *Universal Asynchronous Receiver/Transmitter*
A chip that translates incoming data for the computer and modifies outgoing data for effective transmission.

unbundled
Descriptive of the availability of an individual

unconditional branch

software program that is also sold as part of a package, such as a draw or paint program that is usually a part of a desktop publishing application.

unconditional branch

A program command that directs a move to another location in the program without exception.

See also, *conditional branch*.

undo command

A feature available in some applications that allows the user to undo the last action or series of actions, such as typing or formatting.

uniform spacing

Descriptive of the positioning of a type face in which every character occupies exactly the same space regardless of the width of the character itself.

See also, *proportional spacing*.

uninterruptible power supply

A sophisticated backup power supply that automatically furnishes battery power to a computer system when the primary power source is interrupted, permitting continued operation or an orderly shutdown.

up and running

Descriptive of a computer and its peripherals that are on line and functioning properly.

update

(1) To add new data or alter saved data in order to reflect the most recent information available.

(2) A newer, revised version of a program, often to improve function, or to correct errors in the function of the older one.

UPS See *uninterruptible power supply*.

up time
The period when a computer is on line and functioning properly.

upwardly compatible
(1) Descriptive of features built into a computer to accommodate anticipated newer features.
(2) Descriptive of a computer that permits upgrading, as to a faster chip or improved video board.
(3) Descriptive of a basic program that can be upgraded to a more sophisticated version if desired.

user definable
Of program features, formatting, *hot keys*, etc. that can be set or altered by the user.

user friendly
Descriptive of a computer system or program that is intuitive, making it easier for the user to learn.

user group
A special interest group that meets to share information about a particular program or computers in general.

user hot line
A telephone number provided by an equipment or software manufacturer or dealer through which a user may access technical help.

user's manual See *operating manual*.

utility
A computer program that improves the performance or productivity of a computer or the user.

V

VAFC *VESA Advanced Feature Connector*
A type of video bus architecture for displaying video

validation

images on a computer monitor screen.

validation See *data validation*.

vaporware

Non–existing softwarepromised by a developer, usually in the developmental or testing stage, and discussed in the media as though it were available on the open market.

variable

A symbol or code that represents a value that changes during processing.

variable length field See *field length*.

variable name

A label representing an element that can assume a changing value, such as a range of cells in a spreadsheet.

vector image

A type of graphic image produced by a *draw program* characterized by smooth lines, accurate scaling, and ease of manipulation.

vertical scrolling See *scrolling*.

VESA *Video Electronics Standards Association*

A trade organization formed mainly to standardize graphics display modes for computer monitors.

VESA local bus

A 32–bit local bus standard that enables communication directly with a processor at its rated CPU clock speed.

VGA *Video Graphics Array*

A standard for high resolution display on a color monitor screen.

video accelerator card

An add–on board in the computer that controls and

enhances the display on a·computer screen.

video memory

An area of RAM that stores a video image.

virtual memory

An extension of a computer's *main memory* or *RAM* in a dedicated portion of hard disk storage.

See also, *swap file*.

virtual reality

The simulation of an environment or conditions with the use of a computer.

virus

Unauthorized and unwanted instructions in a computer that disrupt its normal operation, often acquired from downloaded software or that acquired from unconventional sources such as for pirated software.

VL bus See *VESA local bus*.

VMC *VESA Media Channel*

A type of video bus architecture for displaying full motion video at high resolution on a computer screen.

vocabulary

The collection of reserved words that are acceptable for use in a particular programming language.

voice mail

A type of E–mail in which voice messages are stored as digital data.

voice recognition See *speech recognition*.

voice synthesis See *speech synthesis*.

volatile memory

Computer memory that is erased when power is turned off. See also, *RAM*.

volume label

volume label
The name assigned to a hard disk, a floppy disk, or other storage medium to identify it.

VRAM *video RAM*
Random Access Memory employed on a high–performance video card to communicate with the processor and refresh the computer monitor screen at the same time.

W

.WAV *Waveform*
File name extension for files storing recorded sound.

warm boot
A restart of a computer system while it is running and without turning off the system, often occasioned by a program or hardware malfunction that locks up the system or causes it to perform erratically.
See also, *cold boot*.

wavelength synthesis
A technique for generating sound in a computer based on actual recordings of instruments.
See also *FM synthesis*.

wild card
(1) A symbol within a command that represents an unknown such as a search for a file or database record in which only part of a name is known—a wild card symbol is used in place of the unknown data.
(2) A symbol that represents a variable as in a formula used to select a group of like files or database records.

window
A rectangular viewing area on a computer monitor

screen where data is displayed.

Windows®

A **menu–driven** graphical user interface in which programs, directories, and files are indicated by **icons**, and data is displayed in rectangular frames that can be manipulated by the user.

wireless communication

The coupling of computers or peripherals (such as a mouse to a computer) using radio or infrared light rays instead of wires.

.WKS

File name extension for a **spreadsheet** file.

.WMF *Windows Metafile*

A file name extension for a bitmapped image, a type of graphics file.

word processor

(1) A computer program for the writing and editing of text, usually with enhancements that allow special formatting.

(2) A machine similar to a typewriter with a small screen attached that is used solely for word processing. In most cases, the program is built into the machine and cannot be altered. A word processor machine has capabilities beyond that of a typewriter, but somewhat more limited than a word processor program on a PC.

word wrap

A word processor program feature that enables text to overflow to the next line without a carriage return or to flow around a graphic element.

workstation

(1) Any PC, whether stand–alone or attached to a

.WPD

computer network.

(2) An input device attached to a network, usually with a monitor screen, but lacking the ability for independent processing.

.WPD

File name extension for a **word processor** file.

.WPG *WordPerfect Graphics*

A file name extension for a WordPerfect vector image, a type of graphics file.

write protect

A computer program feature that prevents overwriting a file or specified data in the file.

WYSIWYG *What You See Is What You Get*

Descriptive of the representation of type and graphics on a computer screen that closely emulates the image that will be printed.

X

.XLS

File name extension for a **spreadsheet** file.

Z

zap

(1) A program command to clear a monitor screen and start fresh.

(2) To unintentionally delete or overwrite a computer file.

Zero Insertion Force

A computer chip socket that locks the chip in place with a small lever, thus allowing replacement without exerting undue pressure on the motherboard or on the chip itself.

An
Introduction
To
Personal
Computers

The technology that drives computers and their peripherals is changing so rapidly that anything we describe as "state of the art" today will almost surely lose that status within months.

The repeated promises and delivery of newer, faster, or more versatile systems and software makes one hesitant to commit to a system for fear of missing out on something better. Moreover, this constant introduction of new systems tends to drive down the price of the old, so that even when we make a decision to buy, we may be concerned about paying too much for the system we've selected.

And of course there's always the concern about which system is the right one. Do we really need the latest system? Or can we save some money by investing in a less expensive system that is being driven off the market by a newer one? Can we run the programs we use at work as well as those the kids use in school?

In this section we've attempted to address some of those concerns.

First, *Our Romance With Computers* briefly traces the ancestry of computers and offers some insight into the tasks we can reasonable expect to accomplish with today's personal computer. And we explore a few sources where one interested in the latest technology might go for additional information.

Buying a Computer suggests some things that one should consider before purchasing a computer or associated peripheral.

The *Hardware* section features a general, non-technical description of the elements that make up a computer system, some of the optional equipment that can be added to a system, and how they all work (and sometimes don't work) together.

Applications, or the programs that make our computer useful are an extremely important consideration. We've prepared a broad outline of the types and range of applications that are likely to be of general interest, from those that are basic, inexpensive, and generally easy to learn to those with lots of bells and whistles that tend to be more expensive and often more difficult to master.

Managing Your Computer offers some suggestions for ways to get the most out of a computer system.

Contents

INTRODUCTION TO PERSONAL COMPUTERS

Our Romance With Computers

The good news is that most of the things you expect from a computer are achievable

Forerunners of the computer in one form or another have been with us for a long time. The abacus, a hand–held counting device that is still in use throughout the Orient, dates back to about 500 BC The French scientist, Blaise Pascal developed a mechanical calculator in the middle of the 17th century that formed the basis for calculators manufactured well into the 20th century.

Forerunners of the Modern Computer

Credit for the concept of the modern computer goes to the British mathematician Charles Babbage who in the 1830's designed a steam–powered 'analytical engine' that worked with punch cards. Although Babbage worked for decades at perfecting his design, he never built the machine.

In the 1880's, American inventor Herman Hollerith developed a 'tabulator' to manipulate data on punch cards. The device was used to compile data from the 1890 census in less than two months compared to the more than seven years it took to compile data from the previous census by hand!

In 1848 George Boole, another British Mathematician, developed a system of binary logic in which all questions could be answered as "true" or "false". It was almost a hundred years, however, before a computer was developed based on binary numbers using Boolean logic or Boolean algebra.

Until the late 1930's, calculators or computers were based on the decimal system, mechanical devices that required hundreds of moving parts. The transition to binary logic allowed the use of electrical circuitry, that is, switches that were turned on or off, to perform complex calculations.

Electronic Computers

In the early 1940's the electronic computer came into being with the mechanical relays replaced by vacuum tubes. These were, however, single–purpose computers designed to aid in the war effort.

The first general–purpose electronic computer was ENIAC *(Electronic Numeric Integrator and Calculator)* that was put into operation at the University of Pennsylvania in 1946—a 30–ton machine that contained over 17,000 vacuum tubes and performed 100,000 operations per second (100 kilohertz, or KHz), 1000 times slower than today's 100 megahertz (or MHz) chips.

With the invention of transistors in 1948, unreliable vacuum tubes that generated an immense amount of heat were replaced by small transistors that functioned perfectly as switches and generated little heat.

By 1953 there were only about 100 computers in the entire world. They were huge expensive machines and none but a few visionaries anticipated that one day machines that were hundreds of times smaller and thousands of times more powerful would occupy most homes and offices. Thomas J. Watson, Sr., who built IBM into a company that dominated the business–machine industry world–wide is credited with contending that there was a world market for less than a dozen computers!

Personal Computers

The first integrated circuit for computers was developed in 1958. Only in 1971 was the microprocessor that contains all the basic elements of a computer on a single chip introduced, followed by affordable desktop computers in the mid–1970's.

As you can see, the computer as we know it is a relatively recent development. And along with the machine itself, the techniques for programming changed as well. Early computers were built as single–purpose machines, that is, they were built to perform a specific task. The general–purpose ENIAC brought on line in

1946 was programmable, but changing a program required rewiring the machine! Even though later computers retained programs in memory, one needed to be familiar with a host of special codes, commands, syntax, etc. in order to run those programs.

The micromini computers of the 1970's and most in the 1980's followed the same pattern as the early mainframes, that is, they required extensive knowledge of command codes and function keys. Moreover, most required at least some knowledge of programming. After the introduction of the IBM PC in 1981 followed by a host of clones, a greater variety of programs became available, but most still had the look and feel of the mainframe and required some knowledge of operating system commands.

Apple Computer's Macintosh revolutionized the personal computer industry with a machine that shielded the user from the operating system. Called a *graphical user interface* (or GUI), programs, functions, and files are represented by icons or small graphic images that can be selected with a mouse or other pointing device—the user no longer has to memorize an operating system command to load a program or file. In addition, program functions are listed on drop-down menus so that the user is freed from typing commands there as well. And the computer monitor screen has the same appearance for all applications so that learning how to navigate through one application assists one in moving through other applications.

The concept of the graphical interface has been generally described as the most 'user friendly' and has thus been adapted to other operating systems or system interfaces.

Tip: Although we tend to refer to the Macintosh as a 'personal computer' the term originated with the IBM machine introduced in 1981, and PC generally alludes to IBM compatibles.

The only reason for pointing out this difference is that the Mac is in a somewhat different technological world than the PC. Although programs have been written for both the Mac and PC they are, for the most part, not interchangeable; that is, a Mac program will not run on a PC and a PC program will not run on a Mac. The same has been generally true of hardware, although there is a trend toward more compatibility.

Computer Capabilities

Today the micromini computer, whether a desktop, personal computer, laptop, notebook, hand–held, or whatever, has changed our lives. At home we can use a computer to:

- Write a letter or other document
- Maintain a household budget
- Set up and maintain a financial plan
- Track investments

- Shop by modem
- Manage a checking account
- Pay bills
- Maintain a security system
- Check airfare and book passage
- Prepare a tax return
- Keep a household inventory
- Keep an appointment calendar
- Maintain an address book
- Set up and maintain a recipe file
- Access information from remote sources
- Learn a language or other skill
- Play games
- Compose music
- Draw and paint

and at the office to:

- Keep accounting records
- Maintain inventory records
- Record client and personnel data
- Prepare personalized mailings
- Prepare audio-visual presentations
- Publish a newsletter or advertising material
- Compile a catalog

- Track appointments, sales, etc.
- Set up a business plan
- Track projects
- Make labels
- Design buildings, products, etc.
- Project budgets for sales, expenses, etc.

This is only a small sampling of the jobs that can be done with the computer today and doesn't even touch on the things we can expect in the future. More information about some of the programs and techniques is contained in the *Applications* section.

Other Sources of Information

Most of us fall in love with computers in much the same fashion that we fall in love with another person. Unfortunately, both affairs have their ups and downs.

At first meeting, we are enraptured—we fantasize about the ways in which our lives will grow better. A vision of common goals and shared effort carried out in an atmosphere of mutual affection will propel us on gossamer wings to greater achievements. We can sleep late because life will be so much easier. We may even be served breakfast in bed. Then reality rears its ugly head and we learn that the object of our affection has an agenda of its (or her or his) own, and limitations as well. Three minute eggs are not on the menu.

What we're trying to point out here is that despite all the hype about 'user friendly' computers and the ease of 'plug and play' technology, most of us will experience some disparity between our expectations and reality when dealing with computers and applications, especially those that are new to us. There are some things we can do to learn more about computers and keep our expectations reasonable, such as:

- Browsing the stores that sell computers and soliciting opinions on operating systems, software, and the computers themselves from store personnel. Some of these people know little about what they are selling, but you'll be surprised at how many dedicated hackers are selling computers.

- Getting opinions from those you know who use computers at home or at work.

- Looking for information in computer magazines—check the library for back issues, find one that's written in a style you like and at a level you understand, and subscribe to it.

- Attending a meeting of a user's group—these people are serious hackers who take pleasure in sharing information. Most computer stores can put you in touch with a group.

> **Tip:** If your child uses a computer at school, consult with a teacher who has some knowledge about the systems they use. If you expect the child to use the computer at home, you will need to consider acquiring a compatible system or one that can be made compatible.

Keep in mind that most of us are dedicated to a particular type of computer or manufacturer, our operating system, and the programs we use most, so you may have to do some sifting among all the opinions to ascertain which makes the most sense to you.

The good news is that most of the things you expect from a computer are achievable. The not–so–good news is that like any fine romance you have to work at it. Fortunately, romance with a computer is simpler than with a human because computers are so much more predictable.

Buying a Computer

*Buying a computer isn't terribly difficult...
it's simply a matter of weighing
the things you want to do against
the amount of money you have to spend.*

In this section, we'll take a look at some of the things one should consider before deciding on a computer system, including when it may make sense to economize and when it doesn't.

Make a Little List

Of primary importance are your reasons for buying a computer. Make a list of the tasks that could be made easier with the aid of a computer as well some of the things you can't do now, but would like to do. Then consider any special needs that those tasks entail. For example:

• If you want to keep track of personal finances, almost any computer on the market today will do the job, but if you want to receive stock and bond quotations, research a company's earnings performance, or purchase stock with the computer you will need a modem (and a fast one—but more about that later).

- If you plan to bring work home from the office computer, you need to be sure that your home computer is compatible. Same thing if a child is bringing computer files home from school.

- Balancing a checking account or writing letters can be accomplished with a calculator or an inexpensive word processor, respectively. However, if you want to automate the writing of checks or personalize form letters, you need a computer.

- Using a computer for research on the worldwide web requires a modem, but a compact disk drive should be considered as well because of the wealth of material including encyclopedias available on CD-ROM. Most also include sound and support super VGA, but they're not necessary.

- If ya just wanna play games—think hi-tech. The best of today's games require a sound card, speakers, lots of RAM, and a super VGA monitor to view all those great graphics. A joystick or other controller may be required, depending on the program.

Be sure to plan enough tasks for the computer to make the investment worthwhile. If you simply want to learn more about computers in general, consider an adult night class at a local high school or college.

Such a course might help you decide if you really want a computer and if you do, it offers a further opportunity to interact with others and possibly gain some insight into which computer is right for you.

Consider the Cost

Computer systems are available in a wide range of configurations... and prices. So shop around.

- Computer outlets, electronic stores, and office supply stores often offer the best deals, but beware of paying for a lot of bundled software or features that you don't want. Make sure that the store employs knowledgeable personnel who can help if you run into trouble and has a policy of replacement without a fee if a problem cannot be resolved. Few things are so frustrating as to have your new computer sent back to the manufacturer to be tied up for days or weeks.

- Mail order firms generally offer the best prices for high–end machines, and some will configure a computer to your specifications, but be sure the firm has a reputation for reliability, good customer service, and an equitable return policy. Keep in mind that delivery is not immediate and if there are problems, the whole unit may have to be packed up and sent back for evaluation.

- If you know exactly what you want, get advice and prices from a local computer shop that can configure a machine to your specifications. And there is the added advantage that is anything goes wrong you know where to go for help.

There are places where you can save and some where you shouldn't:

- The general admonition is to buy as much power and memory as you can afford in anticipation of future needs. There are exceptions, however:

  - RAM is the fast memory that holds programs and data that you are working on. More RAM means less searching of the hard drive for data, so more RAM generally means more speed... but only up to a point. You probably don't need over 8MB of RAM unless the operating system or programs you plan to run require it. You can usually add more RAM later if you need it, but check with vendor to be sure.

  - Weigh the cost of a large hard drive (over 1 gigabyte) against the cost of an external storage device. Our philosophy has been to limit the hard drive to between 500 and 1000 megabytes, sufficient to hold all of our programs with plenty of space left over. Large data files are then stored on an external device. This provides faster access to the data on the disk; and larger data files, when they are needed, can be quickly downloaded to the hard drive. ...And the external device never runs out of room—we just add another cartridge when we need one.

- If you think you need a compact disk drive, you should get it. Software vendors are increasingly offering their programs on CD–ROM, and even those who offer a choice of CD or 3.5" disks often throw in a lot of extras on the CD that are not available on the 3.5" disks.

- We recommend a high resolution (super VGA) color monitor. For one thing, it's generally easier on the eyes and for another, you'll need it if you plan to view high resolution graphics from a CD or the web. On the other hand, a monitor larger than 14 or 15 inches may not be necessary.

- Printers come in a variety of flavors—impact, laser, inkjet. If high quality or high speed is not important consider a low–priced printer—most vendors can provide a sample sheet that demonstrates the quality of output. Color is fun, but the output of inexpensive color printers often leaves something to be desired. In every case, check out the cost of consumables as they can quickly overshadow the cost of the printer itself.

More about the specifics of equipment on the following pages.

If the computer you select does not include a monitor, be sure to allow for the extra cost. And don't forget the cost of a printer or other device.

Often overlooked is the cost of software. If your computer comes complete with all the bundled software you want, no problem; but if you have to purchase high-end software, the cost of three or four apps can easily double the cost of the computer system.

Depending on how much power you think you need, you may want to search the classified ads for a used computer—great buys are often available when a user decides to upgrade from a machine that is only a year or so old.

Hardware

It's difficult to imagine that just a few decades ago a large room was required to house a computer with only a fraction of the power of today's personal computer that fits on a desktop or in a briefcase. And it took a roomful of money to acquire one of those monstrosities as well.

When the Chips Are Up, the System Hums

The heart of a computer system is the **chip** or **microprocessor**, also called a **CPU** or *central processing unit*. The microprocessor is attached to a motherboard or system board that controls all of the elements that make up a computer system.

Microprocessors come in a variety of flavors, such as the 386 series, 486 series, and Pentium. Chips are differentiated by such things as their clock speed, internal caching, the presence or absence of a math coprocessor, bus size, and the capability for parallel processing.

The **Clock speed** of a chip is calculated in millions of beats or **clock ticks** per second (MHz) such as 486/33 (operating at 33 MHz) or 486/66 (operating at 66 MHz) and is representative of the relative speed at which data is retrieved and processed. Some newer chips are **clock-doubled**, that is, they can retrieve internal data at double the clock speed of that available for external data.

An **internal cache** is a form of fast memory in the chip that stores a copy of frequently used data so that it can be quickly retrieved to speed operations.

A **math coprocessor** is used to perform floating point calculations and markedly speeds up the operation of applications such as drawing or drafting programs that rely heavily on such calculations; some software packages require it. The coprocessor may be built into the main chip or housed in a separate chip. Typically, chips have a suffix (such as DX for built in; SX for not) that indicates the presence or lack of a math coprocessor.

Bus size limits the amount of data transferred in a single pass; the 386 and 486 chips are 32-bit processors, that is, they process 32 bits at a time, while the Pentium is a 64-bit processor. A 64-bit processor, however, will only offer improved performance over a 32-bit processor if the software being run is designed for 64–bit operation.

Parallel processing describes the ability of a chip or chips to process more than one set of instructions at the same time.

It's impractical to recommend a specific product or configuration as new innovations are regularly intro-duced. Suffice it to say that for most home and busi-ness applications, anything currently on the market is more than adequate; for high–powered graphics, real-time video, or multi–tasking, one may need to shop around, especially among users, for their comments.

Tip: If you anticipate using the computer for high–end games, or accessing a multimedia encyclopedia from CD–ROM, buy the best you can afford. At the very least, check the software package for recommended configuration, then go a little better.

Thanks For the Memory

The term *memory* refers to either of two types of computer storage: *volatile memory* such as RAM that needs to be constantly refreshed to be retained; and *static memory* or permanent storage that is re-tained even after the computer is turned off.

RAM, or *Random Access Memory* is volatile memory that is erased when the power goes off. Program instructions and data held in RAM can be accessed and saved much more quickly than that held in permanent storage; therefore, files needed to run a program and data that is being processed are held in RAM while they are in use.

> **Tip:** For the faint of heart, when programs or data files are called up from permanent storage, they are not *moved*, they are merely *copied*. If the power goes off during processing, programs normally are safe; the only loss will be data that was changed since the last save. (On the other hand, if you fear lightning strikes, see **UPS**, below.)

The amount of RAM you need depends at least partly on the **operating system** you select as well as the type of programs you intend to run.

When you boot up the computer, the operating system, or part of it, is loaded into RAM along with a variety of utilities required for normal operation; thereafter, programs and data are loaded into what's left. As little as 2MB (megabytes) total will suffice for most DOS programs. In a Windows® 3.x environment, 4MB is the recommended minimum, but 8MB runs far better. We know some experienced hackers who claim that Windows 95® is a headache even with 16MB. And OS/2® is reputed to be a memory hog as well.

Tip: If your thoughts turn to a MAC, don't worry—it comes loaded with a proprietary operating system and the proper amount of RAM to run it.

Beyond operating system demands, the amount of RAM required depends on the applications to be run— heavy graphics, real–time video, and such need more RAM to keep things from slowing to a crawl. Generally, off–the–rack machines come with 8 to 16MB, more than enough for a general–purpose computer.

Improved handling of memory, reduced access times, and lower cost have conspired to make larger amounts of RAM practical, which in turn has given programmers free rein to add more bells and whistles, and frankly, to get a bit more sloppy by writing programs that require more RAM. There is no reason to believe that the trend will not continue.

As for *static memory*, you don't have to be very old to remember buying a computer without a *hard drive*, then later installing a 20MB hard drive, unable to imagine every needing more storage than that. Today, a 250MB hard drive is a rarity; most new computers are in the 500 to 1000MB (1 gigabyte) range. And you may well need it!

A hard drive or **hard disk** or *fixed disk*—so-called because the drive and disk are an integrated unit—may be installed in the computer case or it may be an external unit. The hard disk is actually a set of disks mounted on a shaft with sufficient space between them to accommodate a read/write head, the unit that reads from and writes to the rapidly spinning disks.

The hard drive is designed to store all of the programs and data that you save.

A 500MB drive costs less today than that 20MB drive cost 10 years ago. And so, as with RAM, programmers feel no compunctions about loading a disk up with all sorts of program files. In all fairness, improved graphics and color (and our desire for them) has to share part of the blame—a simple line drawing can take up 2 KB (kilobyte, 1000 bytes) of space, about the same as a 2 page letter; in color, it may take 200 KB; and a few seconds of real time video can rack up over a megabyte.

The potential problem with a humongous hard drive is that there's little incentive to clean up the disk periodically so that you may be doomed to be overwhelmed by it, unable to find anything you really need. Unless of course you take care to organize your data well. But more about that later...

Not–So–Floppy Disks

So now you have a fast chip, lots of RAM in which to roam (is that a pun?), and scads of room for storing data. Now we need a means to get data in and out of the machine. Still among the most common devices for loading programs and backing up data is the *floppy disk drive*.

Why *floppy disk*? Because the early PC's used 5.25" and larger disks that were indeed thin and floppy. When the 3.5" disk that can hold more data than a 5.25" disk, and that has the added advantage of being rigid and better protected was introduced, the name stuck. So that rigid 3.5" disk is still called a floppy disk. There are four common types of floppy disk still in use:

3.5", high density, holds about 1.4MB of data

3.5", double density, holds about 720KB of data

5.25", high density, holds about 1.2MB of data

5.25", double density, holds about 360KB of data

Don't waste money on a 5.25" floppy disk drive as they are rarely used anymore.

Tip: If you have a collection of old 5.25" disks holding data that you want to save, find someone with a 5.25" drive who can download the data to 3.5" disks for you, then file the larger disks with your 8–track tapes.

Other Removable Media

Despite the ease with which they can be transported, even the venerable 3.5" disks are losing ground. *Compact disks* and other removable media are taking over.

As program data and files become more voluminous, software vendors are replacing sets of ten and twelve 3.5" program disks with a single compact disk that has a capacity in the gigabyte range. All that extra space is a boon for consumers as well—vendors often use the extra disk space to give away clip art and fonts or to include a sampling of other products.

The time is fast approaching when compact discs will also become a likely choice for backing up data as drives that can write to CD's as well as read them become affordable.

There are a variety of drives, disks, and cartridges that use electromagnetic or optical technology, commonly used for backing up and transferring data. Some drives are designed to be mounted in a computer case, others are connected externally and can be moved from one computer to another.

> **Tip:** A *removable drive* offers not only a means to back up a computer's hard disk, but allows the user to unplug the drive and attach it to another computer. A high capacity drive permits one to easily move the entire contents of a computer to a new location.

The configuration of drives, disks, and cartridges is constantly changing as manufacturers strive to increase seek time, transfer rates, and capacity. Cost is also volatile as each manufacturer seeks a niche in the market. Before investing removable media, the are several things that should be considered:

- How much capacity do I need on a single disk or cartridge? Backing up the entire computer system on a regular basis can be a real pain if you have to spend a lot of time switching disks. In addition, backing up everything on a single disk is not only convenient, you may be able to program the computer to back up at regular intervals when the system is not in use. If you only plan on incremental backups or copying files for transfer, a less expensive, smaller capacity device may be adequate to suit your needs.

- If you plan to send data on magnetic media to another location such as to a service bureau to print your output, be sure that the media you select is compatible with the recipient's.

- If you plan to move the drive itself, between office and home for example, be sure that the drive is compatible with both machines.

- If you want to work with programs or data from the removable drive rather than downloading them to the hard drive of the object computer, be sure that access time is fast enough to keep from slowing you down.

- If you plan to select only specific files to download at any given time, be sure the media supports it. Most tapes, for example, do not provide for a selective restore.

Once you've determined the way in which you plan to use the storage device, figure out how much total memory you expect to need. Then calculate the total cost of the drive and the number or disks or cartridges required for each of the systems under consideration to find out which is the best buy.

Ports and Slots

Ports are the connections on the outside of a computer case that permit the exchange of data with an external device. *Slots* are bays in the computer case that are occupied by *add-on boards*, usually with connectors, or bays to which boards may be added in the future (called *open slots*).

Minimally, a computer should come equipped with:

- a special connector to accommodate a keyboard
- a special connector to attach a monitor
- at least one parallel port
- at least one serial port

It may also have connectors for:

- a mouse
- a telephone line
- a gaming device such as a joystick
- speakers
- a microphone or other audio input device
- two or more open slots.

The *monitor connector* (a 15–pin plug receptacle similar in size and shape to the serial port connector) and *keyboard connector* (a round 6–pin plug receptacle) are generally standard, so that almost any monitor or keyboard you buy will come equipped with a plug to fit the respective connectors.

A *parallel port connector* (a 25–pin plug receptacle similar in shape to the serial port connector, but larger) is a multichannel interface that permits the transfer of a full computer word (usually 8 bits or 1 bite) at one time. Usually designated as LPT1 or LPT2, the parallel port is the traditional connector for a printer.

Increasingly, other peripheral devices such as ZIP drives (a removable, high capacity disk drive) are connected through the parallel port. In such cases there is often a pass–through on the device to which a printer can be connected so that the printer is not shut down when the other device is in use.

The *serial port* (a 9–pin plug receptacle similar and very near in size to the monitor connector) as one might imagine, transfers data in series, one bit at a time. Because of the slower rate of transfer as compared to the parallel port, the serial port is customarily used for devices that have less data to transfer. Often a mouse or other input device is connected through the serial port.

The *mouse connection* can be through a serial port (serial mouse) or through a round receptacle similar to that used for the keyboard (a PS/2 mouse, so-called for it's emulation of the connector used by IBM for its Personal System/2 computer). The advantage of a PS/2 mouse is that it frees up the serial port. If the computer does not have a dedicated PS/2 port for the mouse, be sure to buy a serial mouse.

> **Tip:** You can buy a conversion plug that allows connection of a serial mouse to a PS/2 receptacle, but we haven't been able to find one that goes the other way.

> **Tip:** The keyboard and mouse receptacles are similar except in function. If your computer comes equipped with a receptacle for a PS/2 mouse be sure that mouse and keyboard are plugged into the correct slots or they may not function properly.

The *telephone line connection* (a standard telephone jack) provides the means by which data is sent over telephone lines, such as for sending and receiving faxes, communicating with another computer, and exchanging information over the worldwide web. Customarily there are two connectors, one for the incoming telephone line and one that connects to the telephone. If the computer lacks a telephone line connection, chances are it doesn't have an internal modem. But never fear, you can always install an external modem.

The **gaming device connector** (a 15–pin plug receptacle similar to the monitor receptacle) provides for the addition of a joystick or other similar device.

Connectors for **speakers** and **audio input** are customarily a part of a **sound card** that controls all **audio functions** such as output to speakers or headphones and input from a microphone, synthesizer, or other audio device. If the computer lacks these connections, you probably don't have a sound card installed, but they can be added and they're easy to install.

Open slots are important for those things you may want to do in the future. Most of us buy a computer with the idea that it has everything on it that we want or need forevermore. Then a new device comes on the market, or one we crossed off our wish list becomes affordable, and we can't resist the urge to expand. Even a computer configured to your specifications should have at least two open slots for adding a sound card, scanner, or other device.

Input Devices

As noted earlier, removable media such as floppy disks or compact disks are the most common means for loading programs, graphic files, font files, etc. In the section on *Connectivity* we also discuss downloading programs or data from other computers or from a website.

There are a number of other devices commonly used to enter commands, and to enter or manipulate data:

- a keyboard
- scanner
- mouse
- trackball
- pen

Keyboard

The **keyboard** is the primary means for entering unique data into most general–purpose computers. Commonly, we use a standard QWERTY keyboard with letters arranged in the same order as those on a typewriter. (QWERTY are the first six letters in the upper tier of keys.) In addition to the keys found on a standard typewriter, a full–sized computer keyboard contains a number pad, and several command, function, and shift keys.

Computer keyboards have been fairly standard for a number of years. Probably the most significant innovation, resented by many, was to move the function keys from the left side of the board to the top when the number pad was added.

Recent years have seen a number of keyboard innovations, however. Concern about repetitive strain injuries has prompted the introduction of several ergonomic keyboards with keys arranged on a surface that is rounded instead of flat, or segmented keyboards that allow the user to move the left- and right-hand sides farther apart or to position them at an angle on either the horizontal or vertical plane for greater comfort.

The drive for greater utility and portability has led to other innovations such as a keyboard that incorporates a scanner.

Another innovation is a keyboard that contains just one key for each finger—characters are formed by pressing key combinations. Reputedly easy to learn, it may gain wide acceptance one day, especially in special purpose applications.

The action of the keys on some boards is better than on others, but only a very experienced typist is likely to notice the difference.

Tip: If you often need access to non–standard characters, such as letters with foreign language accent marks, a copyright symbol, or fractions, consider setting the keyboard to U.S. International which allows access to a variety of symbols through the right side Alt key. You can use a character set utility such as the one in Windows, but it's inconvenient if you have to access it often.

Incidentally, the QWERTY keyboard is a carryover from the days of mechanical typewriters and was designed to prevent a fast typist from locking up the keys. One who is not already a touch typist and doesn't have to use a number of different computers may prefer the *Dvorak Simplified Keyboard,* a keyboard in which the letters are arranged to make typing easier and faster. Although acclaimed by its users, the Dvorak keyboard will probably never completely replace its more familiar rival.

Scanner

Scanners have become increasingly common to satisfy our thirst for more graphics and to aid in our quest for the paperless society. They have become more accessible as well, ranging from small, hand–held devices to full–page units complete with document feeders.

The ability to add images to a graphics library, to save and manipulate the photos in a personal album, to escape tedious keyboarding by scanning in pages of copy, or to replace mountains of archived office files with a small box of backup disks have all fueled the desire for scanners.

Tip: Be careful that you don't infringe on someone else's copyright by scanning and reproducing material that is proprietary.

Some of the considerations that enter into the choice of a scanner are:

- flatbed or portable
- resolution; the fineness of the image
- monochrome or color

Flatbed scanners generally offer the highest resolution with the greatest versatility and ease of use—simply place the copy to be scanned on the glass, close the flap, set the controls, and scan—similar to using an office copy machine. To scan a large number of papers, you simply attach a document feeder, available as an option for most flatbed scanners.

Choose a flatbed scanner if you anticipate heavy usage or expect to scan full page images at high resolution. They come in a wide range of prices, from a few hundred to several thousand dollars. Most flatbed scanners require an open slot in the computer case for installation of a controller board, generally a relatively easy task. If you are not comfortable playing around inside the computer, find a vendor who will install it as well for a reasonable fee.

Handheld scanners can be a challenge, as they rely on the user's ability to move slowly across an image with a steady hand. Some make allowances for slight wavering, and we've seen inexpensive devices that help hold the scanner in line, but it can still be a daunting task.

The handheld does have it's advantages, however:

- generally lower cost than a flatbed

- requires a minimum of desk space

- greater portability and connectivity if it is one that hooks up to a parallel port and does not require a special board

If you only need to input a few lines of copy now and then such as scanning business cards or letterheads to add to your address book, or if you occasionally want to add small images to your graphics library, by all means, consider a handheld.

Somewhere between the two are the ***roller scanners*** that either connect to a computer's parallel port or that require their own board, depending on the unit. Almost as portable as a handheld (about 11" wide by

3" deep by 3" tall), a roller scanner has the advantage of accepting a single page and feeding it between two rollers which makes it ideal for those of us who do not have a steady hand.

Resolution refers to the fineness of scan of an image. We tend to think of it in relation to fine halftones or color images, but it can be important when scanning type as well. Small type or type that is poorly printed or faded can be better scanned at a high resolution.

You probably won't need 1200 dpi—dots per inch, a measure of the fineness of an image; the higher the number, the finer the image—unless you are creating a commercial product that requires extremely subtle gradations of black and white or of color.

A resolution of 400 or 600 dpi is adequate for most tasks; avoid the limitations of 300 dpi, especially for optical character recognition (more about that below) unless you are confident that is all you will need.

Tip: Keep in mind that the finer the resolution, the longer an image takes to scan and the larger the resultant image file. Extremely high resolution scanning may also call for more RAM—a total of 32 to 64MB.

The decision to buy a **monochrome** (black and white) or **color scanner** depends on intended use as well. Color scanners are quite affordable, and generally a better choice than a plain vanilla monochrome scanner, but not all color scanners are created equal, so be sure to get one adequate to the tasks you intend for it.

If you have no immediate plans to scan in color, consider one of the lower priced color scanners just to give you the flexibility if you need it in the future.

Most scanners come with software that allows the user to set the resolution at which the image is to be scanned, permits selection of color or black and white, and provides for manipulation of the final image. Many provide settings to adjust for contrast (or lack thereof) and brightness (slick paper may produce random dots) of the original; some will ignore 'background noise' or random dots on the original.

Scanners are increasingly being used in offices to archive files. In some cases, once the documents are scanned, the originals are destroyed. In situations where the original must be kept to satisfy a legal requirement, the scanned file can be used to create copies without searching through dusty archives. The file can also be used to quickly locate the original when it is needed.

There are software programs available that can assist in the storage, sorting, cataloging compression, and management of archived documents.

Another software application, **OCR (Optical Character Recognition)**, should be considered at this point as well. Data captured with the use of a scanner is saved as a graphic image—optical character recognition is the system for identifying those graphic images that represent characters and translating them into text that can be manipulated from the keyboard.

Used extensively to copy documents for editing, OCR can be a tricky business. Almost any program will suffice to translate a clearly typewritten or printed document scanned at 300 dpi. However, if the image varies in density or brightness, or if the characters are very small, 400 or even 600 dpi scanning may be necessary in order for the program to achieve a satisfactory hit ratio in identifying the characters. Some of the more expensive programs have a learning capability, that is, whenever a character or combination of characters is marked as having been improperly identified, the program adjusts its matrix so as to properly identify it on future reads.

Pointing and Selecting

Just as the scanner can free us from the chore of typing a document, many other tasks performed on the computer can be speeded up by using a device other than the keyboard. These devices are used to quickly select commands, to highlight text or graphics for manipulation, and to copy or move parts of a document from one place to another.

Mouse

The *mouse* is a hand–held mechanical device with buttons on top and a loosely–held ball on the bottom. Movement of the mouse on a flat surface moves the ball which in turn controls movement of a cursor on the monitor screen. In addition to moving the cursor, the mouse can be used to select text or commands and to manipulate data on the screen by clicking the primary button. A mouse may also have one or two programmable buttons that can be used to execute commands.

Most users begin with the common two–button mouse, usually one that comes with the computer they buy. There are, however, other options that catch their fancy—a three–button mouse, for instance, or one that offers finer resolution.

Only time will tell if you can make use of a more sophisticated mouse. Some applications assign a command to the secondary button. A programmable mouse allows the user to select from a list of commands and assign a key or key combination to execute the command regardless of the active program. For example, although the left mouse button is customarily the one used to click or double–click on an item, some users program the second or third button to emulate a double–click because it is such a common action. A button in combination with one of the shift keys (Control, Alt, or Shift) may also be used to call up a frequently used utility such as a notepad, calendar, or calculator.

Finer resolution means that the cursor moves further on the screen in relation to the distance that the mouse is moved on the desktop. A 300 dpi mouse, for example, will move the cursor from one side of a 17–inch monitor to the other while moving little more than an inch on the desktop—a real boon to those of us who use the mouse a lot.

Naturally, when you drag a mouse about you also drag the cord that attaches it to the computer. If dragging the cord is a drag (sorry about that), check out a *cordless mouse*, one that communicates with the computer via infrared or radio waves.

Trackball

The ***trackball*** functions in much the same fashion as a mouse, but the ball is manipulated from the top by turning it with the palm of the hand. The trackball is especially practical for a laptop of notebook computer, whether built in or attached to the side of the case, because it doesn't require a flat surface to operate.

The desktop unit is usually somewhat larger than a mouse but because it is stationary it doesn't require as much desktop space. The ball for a desktop unit is generally larger than the one customarily found in a mouse; those in laptop or notebook computers are likely to be considerably smaller.

Pen and Pad

Use a ***light pen*** to select commands or to write on a special monitor screen.

Special monitor screens called '***touch–sensitive***' allow you to use your finger as a pen or stylus to select commands or options.

Sensitized pads range from:

- small (about 2" square) units that permit the use of a stylus or finger to move the cursor on a monitor screen, to...

- larger (about 4" by 6") that *are* the screen for a small computer and accept input written to the screen from a digitized pen.

The smaller units are most practical as a stand-in for a mouse on a notebook or laptop computer, or wherever there is limited desk space. The larger units are usually a part of a **PDA (Personal Digital Assistant)**. More about those in the section, *Taking Your Act On the Road.*

Monitors

Consider the monitor screen your workspace. Commands and data are displayed and manipulated on the monitor screen. And the user has a variety of options to consider:

- Monochrome or color

- VGA or super VGA

- Size

- Refresh rate

- Dot pitch

- Screen controls

The first option is an easy one: buy color! Color is very affordable and much easier on the eyes than black and white.

Buy super VGA if you can afford it and your computer's video board supports it. Super VGA offers finer resolution options than VGA and although VGA is more than adequate for word processing or other office tasks, you will need super VGA to view high–resolution graphics, much of the research material offered on CD–ROM, or to play high–end games.

Computer monitors are commonly furnished with 14– or 15–inch screens which is adequate for most uses, but don't be misled; the size isn't the width of the screen, it's a diagonal measurement. In addition, the extreme edges of the screen are likely covered by the case which makes the exposed screen area even smaller. And some screen don't carry the image to the very edge, further reducing the viewable area. So let the buyer beware—look for specifications that give the actual viewing area, text the monitor to make sure that the image extends all out to the extreme edges.

A larger screen is necessary if one wants to view several documents at once or to get a reasonably sized image at a very high resolution. Such luxury comes at a price, however; upgrading from a 15–inch to 17–inch screen can double the cost of a monitor.

A desktop monitor screen is commonly a cathode–ray tube (CRT) that creates an image by firing beams of electrons at a phosphorescent coating on the inside of the tube. As the individual phosphors are struck they emit a burst of light. When the phosphors are struck repeatedly at a rate of 60 times per second or faster, the burst appears to be a steady image. This is called the *refresh rate*.

Although a refresh rate of 60 Hz (hertz, or cycles per second) is common, a higher rate, up to 72 Hz may be necessary to prevent a flickering image. If possible, set your sights on a monitor that supports a variety of refresh rates, or at least the highest rate that your computer's video card supports.

Dot pitch is the distance between the phosphor dots of a given color on the screen of a CRT. Suffice it to say that the smaller the number, the sharper the image. A dot pitch of 0.28 mm. is adequate for most uses; 0.26 mm. is somewhat sharper and often affordable.

Tip: Don't buy a computer monitor sight unseen. Despite knowing what to look for, the best test is what looks right to you. Have a salesperson show you how the image appears at a variety of settings.

Finally, check the controls. They should be easily accessible, preferably at the front of the machine. You should be able to adjust the image for brightness and contrast, to center on the screen, and to entirely fill the screen. In addition, make certain there is no color or image distortion.

Printers

Printers that allow us to present the results of our work to the world also offer a variety of options:

- Dot matrix

- Laser

- Ink jet

- Color or monochrome

A **dot matrix printer** forms characters on a page according to patterns set for each character. The resolution of a 24-pin printer is not going to fool anyone into thinking you have a laser, especially if you try to print graphics or a fine–serif typeface, but it handles straight text well.

Dot matrix printers don't get very much publicity anymore as vendors hype the newer technologies, and it's understandable, because the printer itself and its consumables are the least expensive of any printer. In addition to handling text well, it will outperform other types of printers for some jobs. Near letter quality (NLQ) or typewriter emulation from a 24–pin printer is satisfactory for normal correspondence and the printing speed in draft mode puts a laser to shame.

If you intend to print continuous forms such as checks or long accounting reports, the dot matrix printer is your best choice.

A *laser printer* uses, you guessed it, laser technology to create an image that is transferred to a carrier, such as paper or film. The laser can't be beat for high resolution graphics and text. Prices have come down so that some low–end laser printers costs only about twice as much as a dot matrix.

Tip: When considering the price of a laser, check out the cost for consumables as well—toner cartridges and replacement drums can be expensive.

As with most other hardware, lasers come in different flavors. They may be capable of printing at 300, 400, 600, or 1200 dpi. Anyone preparing output for reproduction should consider a 600 dpi printer; a resolution of 300 or 400 dpi is adequate, but 600 guarantees that no compromises will be made when reproducing a fine line typeface or graphic image. Some manufacturers also have proprietary systems for smoothing images so that 300 dpi output is not the same for all printers.

Tip: If you expect to require laser quality only occasionally, consider using a copy shop or service bureau for your laser printing. Most have high resolution printers that can output from PostScript files. Check with the vendor for exact specifications, but generally you can assign the printing to a PostScript printer, then print to a file to take to the copy shop or service bureau.

A laser printer can also transfer images to film, a handy option if much of your work goes directly to a printer. Most service bureaus can accommodate output to film as well.

Ink jet technology that creates an image by spraying (you guessed it again) tiny jets of ink, has come a long way. All of those we know with ink jet printers are thrilled with their choice, but frankly we're not all that impressed with the output. Perhaps from one of the more expensive models...

As with the laser, consider the cost of consumables as well as the price of the printer.

Despite the introduction of some reasonably priced *color printers*, monochrome still dominates the market. A color printer can be fun, however, and if one wants to make up special presentations, it may even be necessary.

Here again, consider the cost of consumables as well as the cost of the printer itself. Check too, to see if the colors are sold and loaded individually—if the colors are packed as a unit, you may have to buy the whole thing even though only one color has been depleted.

Tip: As with a monitor, try before you buy. Most printers are set up with a test program that provides a sample of the quality of output.

Multimedia

Multimedia describes the use of a combination of sensory elements, often to entertain or to educate. As CPU's become faster and more powerful, they are better able to accommodate presentations that include combinations of sophisticated sound, graphics, and video. For example, a computer encyclopedia may include a short video that shows an animal in its natural habitat complete with ambient sounds or a voice–over narration, or both; an entry about music may show a full orchestra playing and then introduce each of the instruments with samples of the sound it makes. A software application may include an introduction or a tutorial that uses sound and animation to illustrate program features.

Multimedia isn't limited to presentations that are a part of commercial software—there are programs that enable users to create and combine music, narration, and videos for their own use. Beyond the entertainment value of these programs, they are useful in business to design presentations, such as to introduce a new product; to prepare reports where a video can best illustrate a point; or to train new employees. And a sound stage or studio isn't required to create them.

So–called *multimedia computers* come equipped with a CD–ROM drive, a sound card with speakers, and perhaps a microphone and scanner for input. This pre-packaged equipment is normally adequate for those of us who simply want to play a few games, have access to the full capabilities of a multimedia encyclopedia, and occasionally insert a sound bite or some graphics in a text file or report.

Tip: Even an off–the–shelf computer sound card should be compatible with a broad range of applications. If there is any doubt, check out the sound card's documentation or test your software before you buy.

Those who wish to record and play back serious music or videos, however, may need to consider more sophisticated equipment than that normally bundled with a compute. Check out these add–ons carefully, and wherever possible, try before you buy.

• Make certain that the host computer is sufficiently powerful and has enough RAM to run multimedia programs seamlessly, that is, without any hesitation or jerkiness in the either the sound or picture;

• Be sure that the sound card is the right one for you. A card that is adequate for voice synthesis will prove disappointing for use with high–tech games or for music synthesis. Check to see that the card is configured to work with your hardware as well—a MIDI–compatible sound card, for example, designed to produce sounds from a keyboard or synthesizer, requires a MIDI adapter in order to connect with an external device; some units can only reproduce sounds from a synthesizer that is built into the card.

• Speakers should be shielded and designed for use with a computer system.

• Affirm that the graphics card is able to display at the quality level you require and that it is compatible with the monitor. To speed up the display of business graphics, an accelerator card that displays 256 colors should be adequate; photo manipulation requires 24–bit color at higher resolutions. Local bus accelerators perform the best, but call for a system equipped with a local bus connector.

You will probably want to check out a CD drive that records as well, because an elaborate presentation will require a lot more memory than a floppy disk can hold, and the access time for a CD is less, so that the program will run better.

Connectivity

Around the Office or Home...

A LAN or **Local Area Network** is used to connect a number of computers or workstations to a base computer or file server and peripherals such as printers throughout an office. Setting up, configuring, and managing a LAN can be complicated and so most companies that have one installed employ a resident guru or outside consultant to control it. If you plan to connect to an office LAN from a home or portable computer, it's best to check with the administrator to find out about any special hardware requirements before you buy.

A **peer-to-peer network**, although not as sophisticated as a LAN, provides the means to connect a limited number of computers simply and economically. Installation requires a special add-on board for each of the computers that are to be connected, sufficient cable to connect them, and software to run the program. Installed the boards and setting up the software is generally uncomplicated as long as there are no special programs or devices on either computer that can cause a conflict; even then, most are easily resolved.

The network permits the exchange of interoffice mail or messages, and although each computer can be allowed to access data from another, the link can be restricted; that is, access to certain files or programs may be limited or prevented by locking them out. On the down side, single–user programs can be accessed by only one user at a time so that a controller can't print a financial report while a bookkeeper is making entries in the accounting program, for example.

...And Around the World

Important to many users is the ability to communicate with others at a distance, whether by E-mail, voice mail, fax, or on the Internet.

Any communication over telephone lines requires a fast, reliable modem. The modem, from MOdulator/DEModulator, is a device that translates computer digital signals to signals that can be carried over telephone lines and then back again to computer digital signals. Speed is important, especially if files to be transmitted are large or if transmission is carried over long distance lines, in the interest of saving both time and money.

Tip: Regardless of how fast your modem is, transmission speed is limited to the slowest link in the chain between your computer, the telephone lines, and the receiving device. Solutions to the problem of the large number of users on the Internet clogging the system is increasingly concentrated on those devices that limit transmission speeds, so you can be reasonable assured that speeds will increase. Buy the fastest unit you can, and, if possible, buy one that can be upgraded. You will save in the long run.

A modem can be internal, that is, contained entirely in the computer, whether built into the computer case or installed as an add–on into one of those open slots we described earlier; or it can be external, connected for example to a PCMCIA or PC card slot.

Both data communication (E–mail, Internet, or some other on–line service) and fax require special software to run them. Opt for software that controls both in order to avoid conflicts that require resetting the modem after you use it.

Tip: Sending a fax requires an extra conversion from digital data to a graphic image and, if the material is to be edited by the recipient, it must be converted by an OCR program back to text that can be manipulated in a word processor or other program. When communicating with another computer, transmission is faster and simpler if the material is sent as a data file.

Some modems, with the appropriate software, can provide voice mail capabilities similar to those of an answering machine with the ability to answer calls, play an outgoing message or announcement, and record incoming messages.

Personal Digital Assistant

The PDA is another means of getting connected. The device is essentially a hand–held computer designed to hold an address book, appointment calendar, and some stripped down versions of PC programs such as a spread sheet in addition to communications software. The PDA enables the user to send and receive faxes or E–mail, surf the net, and to connect with a home or office computer.

Features vary from one device to another, such as:

• size and weight—some PDA's are truly hand–held while others are somewhat more than a handful;

• a tiny keyboard for entering data versus an on–screen keyboard that is activated with a stylus;

• handwriting recognition that allows the user to enter data by writing on the screen pad;

• a built–in modem versus an external modem; and

- more support by independent hardware and software developers whose devices and programs provide a wider range of options to the user.

A PDA is certainly not a replacement for a PC, but if you spend a lot of time on the road, and your main concern is keeping in touch, this small, lightweight solution may be the one for you.

Taking Your Act On the Road

If you move around a lot and a PDA (see above) just doesn't do everything you want to do when you're away from your PC (see above), there are alternatives, such as a laptop or notebook computer.

There doesn't seem to be a firm delineation between a laptop and a notebook computer except that notebooks tend to be more compact than laptops, and often have an undersized keyboard. For our purpose here, we'll simply call them both *portables*.

For those of us who rely on the computer for running our lives, the concept of taking our computer wherever we go is certainly appealing. There are likely to be a number of differences between this diminutive package and the desktop PC we use every day, however, which we need to consider before we buy:

- Monitor screen

- Keyboard

- Connectors

- Memory

- Storage

- Upgrading and expanding

Monitor Screen

The monitor screen of a portable computer is likely to be smaller, and often much smaller, than a desktop monitor. This may be a problem for some, especially one who is accustomed to working with more than one window visible on the screen at the same time. A variety of screen sizes are available, however, so keep that in mind when selecting a portable computer.

Quality of the screen image varies, as well, often affected by ambient light. Be sure that the screen can be set to an angle that affords comfortable viewing in any lighting condition.

Width of the viewing angle can vary considerable from one screen to another; a wide viewing angle is important if more than one person needs to see the screen at the same time, such as for a sales presentation.

Keyboard

A keyboard that is slightly smaller than a conventional keyboard may be disconcerting to a fast typist, but probably won't bother most of us. Even a hunt-and-peck typist, however, may have difficulty with a keyboard that is a lot smaller.

Consider, too, the placement of keys. We've found keyboards on portables with the tilde (~) and backslash (\) keys in unusual places, but as they are seldom used, it posed no special problem. Placement of the *Delete* and *Insert* keys to the right of the space bar where *Alt* and *Ctrl* keys are traditionally placed posed a serious problem, however. And where were the right side *Alt* and *Ctrl* keys? There weren't any! Doesn't seem very important, but we soon realized how intuitive some of our moves are when we inadvertently inserted or deleted material instead of executing a hot key command. The *Enter* and *Shift* keys that are used a lot should also be in their customary position—with that errant backslash key placed next to the right side *Shift* key, shifting required an extra stretch, and we often missed.

It's tough to judge the influence of the action of the keys or even key placement on your typing after only a brief tryout at the store, but if it's important to you, pull up a word processor and type a page of notes about the computer you intend to buy. It should give you some idea of how the keyboard responds to the way in which you work.

Those whose work involves a lot of numbers may also miss the number pad on an expanded keyboard. If this is the case with you, check to see if the portable you are considering will permit the addition of a separate number pad.

Connectors

A portable should have both a serial and parallel port as well as a 3.5" or CD drive. Be sure that the drive you select is suited to your needs—a CD drive may seem attractive playing your favorite game or viewing the contents of an encyclopedia, but if the application programs you want to use are only available on 3.5" disks...

Most portable computers have ports for connecting a separate monitor, a mouse, or an enhanced keyboard. If you want that flexibility—see *Desktop or Portable?*, below—be sure to check it out. And be sure that the external monitor connector supports the resolution you require.

PCMCIA or *PC Card* slots, about the size of a credit card, but thicker, are commonly installed in portables for adding an external drive or modem. There are three types of PC Cards, however, and not all are compatible, so review the documentation that comes with the computer to be sure the connector can handle all three. In addition, before you buy a PCMCIA device, insist that you be allowed to try it out to be sure that it works with your computer.

If the computer has a built-in modem or fax, there should also be connectors for a telephone line.

Memory

A portable computer's RAM is essentially the same as that installed in a desktop computer. In the past, when RAM was very expensive and only top of the line portables were expected to match the power of a desktop computer, prices were kept down by limiting the amount of installed memory. As RAM prices dropped and user expectation grew, the amount of installed RAM and expandability increased.

Storage

The data storage area, a computer's hard drive, is also fundamentally the same as that found on a desktop computer. The physical dimensions early hard drives was a limiting factor in older portables; today's hard drives have been miniaturized sufficiently to rival the capacity of those installed in most desktops. And if that isn't enough, there are a number of external drive solutions that can fill almost any user's needs.

Desktop or Portable?

As portables grow increasingly more powerful, many users consider them the one size that fits all. Those who prefer a larger monitor screen or an enhanced keyboard whenever they are available can set up a workstation at home or in the office with those devices on hand to be plugged into the portable.

For the ultimate in convenience, there are portables, albeit pricey ones, that come with a docking station—a full–size monitor and keyboard are attached to the station so that when the portable itself is nested and plugged into the station, the setup becomes indistinguishable from a desktop system.

Power Management

The small size, relatively light weight, and self–contained power source of a laptop or notebook computer screams mobility: a day of sunning oneself at the beach while turning out productive work. But there are limitations...

Battery power will allow operation of the computer at full force for only a few hours. Most units, however, are designed to extend that time by automatically dimming or blanking the screen, the biggest drain on power, after a specified period of inactivity. Some will power down completely, and come to life only when the user presses a key or moves a pointing device. If you expect to use the computer where AC power is not accessible, check out the power management features carefully. And buy an extra battery.

A battery–operated portable will sound a series of audible beeps when the power begins to run down, allowing sufficient time to save your work and shut down in an orderly fashion, to change batteries, or to find the nearest electrical outlet.

> **Tip:** You probably already know that all batteries are not created equal—some need to be drained completely in order to fully recharge. Keep in mind that most units trickle charge the battery when the computer is plugged into an AC outlet, so that if you often switch between AC and battery, the battery may never be fully charged. Best to get the type of battery that will recharge fully from any state, however, if you get stuck with a battery that doesn't, change your work habits to allow the battery to drain completely whenever you use it.

There is also a limit to the number of times a battery can be recharged, so be prepared to invest in a new one when the operating time on the battery you are using diminishes noticeably.

Upgrading and Expanding

We're inclined to add more memory, a larger hard drive, or a new device to our desktop computer when we need it, but we're not as confident about the ability to do so with a laptop or notebook.

The physical contents of a portable computer are so carefully designed to fit in a tightly packed case that there is virtually no standardization of components between manufacturers and often very little among different models made by a single manufacturer. As a result, most upgrading of portables is limited to the addition of more RAM.

Except for the addition of RAM, upgrading or expanding a portable is generally limited to those devices that can be attached externally.

Portable Scanners and Printers

Time was when the only way to add a scanned image to a portable computer during those periods that the user was traveling was via fax. The ready availability of hand–held and roller scanners has changed all that. Today the user can easily find a scanner that will fit in his or her pack with the computer.

Printing a computer–generated document while on the road presented a similar challenge in the past, with few solutions: send a fax, download the data to a home or office computer via modem, or search out a service bureau with a compatible printer. Some of today's printers, however, have gone through a metamorphosis similar to that of scanners, from large and decidedly not portable devices to a configuration somewhat like a roller scanner that can be easily carried in a briefcase. And there are portable computers available with built–in printers, as well. Now if we only had room in our case for a few sheets of paper...

UPS

In the world of computers, *UPS* stands for *Uninterruptible Power Supply,* a battery backup that sounds a warning when AC power is interrupted and allows sufficient time for an orderly shutdown of a computer.

How important is a UPS? It all depends on what you are doing. Without a UPS, a loss of power signals the loss of all data entered since the last save and, unless you save your work often, you could lost quite a bit. Although it may be no more than a minor inconvenience to reenter data to an accounting program or spreadsheet, think about how it would feel to lose a complex drawing or a page of deathless prose that was painstakingly constructed over a period of hours.

Tip: Don't confuse a *surge protector* or *line conditioner* with a UPS. A surge protector is designed to guard against power spikes that can cause damage to a computer or corrupt data. A line conditioner offers protection against surges as well as against drops in voltage (brownouts) that can damage equipment over time. Their effectiveness varies depending on how sensitive they are and how quickly they react. We use a good quality single plug surge protector for such things as the television and stereo; anyone living or working in an area that suffers from frequent brownouts should consider a line conditioner.

An *orderly shutdown* involves saving open files and closing them, then closing down any applications that are running. An untimely abort or shutdown can cause not only a loss of unsaved data, but in some systems an accumulation of no longer useful temporary files that were used by an application when it was running.

Tip: Regardless of how good a surge protector, line conditioner, or UPS is for protection against a power surge or power loss, it will most likely fry if struck during an electrical storm. For that reason you may want to consider a moderately priced UPS that comes with an insurance policy—any equipment properly connected to the UPS is insured for its replacement value in the event of damage.

Software

The term *software* is used to describe any program, application, routine, etc. that is added to the computer to perform a particular function. Software falls into a number of categories, such as:

- Operating System

- Applications

- Utilities

- Security

Software is required to operate certain peripherals, that is, to interpret commands so that the computer can communicate with the device. For example, some printers and most scanners come with a disk containing a program that has to be installed in order for the device to properly understand commands from the computer and to allow programs to take full advantage of the device's capabilities. In most cases, installation of proprietary software is a relatively simple task that involves accessing the drive where the device's program is stored, usually the A: or B: drive and typing a command such as 'setup' or 'install'.

Operating Systems

An **operating system** is required to manage the computer and enable it to communicate with peripherals such as a monitor, keyboard, mouse, or printer; and to control the flow of commands and data to and from programs or applications.

The predominant operating system in use today is MS–DOS, or *MicroSoft–Disk Operating System*, commonly referred to as DOS. There are, in addition, other versions of DOS that generally function with the same software applications as MS–DOS.

Perhaps a brief (and oversimplified) explanation of the popularity of DOS and hence of PC compatibles is in order here: Those who controlled DOS were amenable to the development of new hardware and software that would work with their operating system, and thus assisted other developers in making their products compatible. The result was a host of clones that not only provided a multitude of options for PC users, but brought prices of the PC's and their peripherals down. The resulting popularity that created a broad base of users further encouraged software developers to seek a niche in this lucrative market.

In general, early users fell into two categories—those who sought ease of use and who were willing to pay for it; and those who opted for lower cost and a broader selection of hardware and software. Lower cost and a host of options won out.

The several versions of Windows are *environments* that offer a graphics interface with the DOS operating system. Debate continues as to whether Windows95 is truly a distinct operating system because although the operating system and graphic environment are incorporated into a tight package, Windows95 functions on a DOS platform. That is to say that the user can access DOS from within Windows95, a proper concession to those who still have DOS programs that they want to utilize, but the system also permits the user to boot up in the DOS environment.

There are other operating systems such as OS/2 and Warp, but none have achieved the popularity of DOS. Although some function with most DOS applications and utilities, they do not function well with all of them, a serious consideration when contemplating a change. And of course the MAC has its own operating system that requires programs specifically designed to work with it.

Keep in mind, however, that all of the operating systems with a broad base of users have their merits and 'most popular' does not mean absolutely right for everyone. Operating system software is not terribly expensive, so you can be reasonably sure that anyone using a particular operating system does so because he or she is satisfied with it. As you talk to other users you will undoubtedly find as well that users can be extremely attached to their systems and not at all shy about extolling the virtues of all their favorite programs as well as the shortcomings of others. It's a great learning experience.

Applications

Applications are the programs designed to perform those tasks that make your computer truly useful. Application packages fall into a number of categories, such as:

- Desktop Publishing
- Word Processing
- Database Programs
- Spreadsheets
- Integrated Software
- Paint & Draw Programs
- Communications
- Multimedia Programs

This delineation between applications often becomes muddled, however, as most are capable of a variety of tasks. For example, desktop publishing programs often duplicate some of the simpler tools found in a paint or draw program; a word processing program may perform many of the functions of a desktop publishing or spreadsheet program; and many spreadsheet programs can be used to set up and manage a database.

Desktop Publishing

Desktop publishing programs are designed to prepare copy for space ads, flyers, publications, and the like. These programs are extremely flexible in their provisions for laying out a page, such as for headlines, placement of marginal heads, creation of columns, etc. Most offer relative ease in the importation and placement of text; allow text to flow through a document; support a variety of text fonts, sizes, and styles; and may even permit the rotation of headlines or graphics. Graphics can be imported, scaled, cropped, and, in some cases, edited from within a document. The programs provide for the creation of headers and footers such as running heads, graphics, or folios that appear on every page.

Most desktop publishing features are focused on graphics, however, and are not designed to set and edit text nearly as well as a word processing program which is why this book was prepared using the latter. A high–end desktop publishing program can do marvelous things, but our experience has been that we don't need most of them, and the difficulty in learning to use the program seems to be in direct proportion to the price.

> **Tip:** Unless you need a particular feature or features offered by a high–end (read that 'expensive') program, opt for an inexpensive one. There are inexpensive programs whose output for most tasks can't be distinguished from that of programs costing four times as much. Or, if you expect to be dealing mainly with text, consider a good word processing program.

Word Processing

Word processing programs were originally designed to merely create text documents, a function formerly relegated to the typewriter. Over time the programs have became more sophisticated, however, incorporating so many of the features of a publishing program that sometimes the two are barely distinguishable from one another.

The basic program for creating a document file is a *text editor* that saves its contents without formatting. The text editor is commonly used to record information that needs to be easily read by or imported into another system. Simple program instructions, for example, are saved as unformatted text.

A true word processing program has its own set of embedded commands, reserved words, or symbols for creating formatting such as to specify a font, line spacing, or indents, and the commands are generally different from one program to another. Saving a file as unformatted text assures that all of the information in the document is readable as text—there are no special commands that can be misinterpreted.

Most operating systems have their own text editor that can be used to write or alter program instructions, and most word processing programs provide the means to save a file as unformatted text, often called an ASCII file. (ASCII stands for American Standard Code for Information Exchange; ASCII symbols are the set of printed and control characters defined by the ASCII standard and that can be understood by most computer systems.)

Lacking the capability to alter the look of a document limits the usefulness of a text editor in preparing such things as letters or reports. To be truly serviceable, a word processor needs much more.

In a non–graphics environment, a program is subject to many of the same restrictions as a typewriter, that is, a finite selection of type sizes and styles, and a limited ability to alter line spacing, letter spacing, indents, etc. In addition, when special typefaces are available, they often cannot be viewed on the screen so that the only way to adjust the position of elements in a document is to print it out, make corrections, and hope for the best at the next printing.

Some early attempts to overcome those restrictions were largely successful, but cumbersome, often requiring that fonts be selected before typing a document then downloaded to the computer for viewing on the screen and downloaded to the printer for printing out the final document. The somewhat accurate emulation of type or graphics on the screen is called WYSIWYG, What You See Is What You Get.

All of this is not to discourage one from using a non–graphics program, but to point out its limitations. On the other hand, if:

- The letters we write are printed out on company stationery, so straight text is all that we need;

- Our memos and reports don't require any graphics or special heads, so ordinary text fills the bill here as well;

- We only need a program that allows us to set up margins, indents, and tabs, to set lines of type single– or double–spaced, and to imitate boldface or italics;

- We may need to set headers and footers that repeat on every page, and even number the pages;
- We may need a spell checker to make final corrections; and
- We want to be able to print a long document quickly in draft mode or more slowly to emulate the quality of typewriter output.

If this roughly describes the tasks you undertake with a word processing program, you don't need the capabilities of an expensive graphics program.

But the graphics interface, on either the MAC or the PC does make quite a change in the way we work and in the look of our output. In a graphics environment, or GUI (Graphical User Interface), the monitor screen image offers a reasonable facsimile of elements as they will be printed. Printed text is a picture element constructed from a set of matrixes or models programmed to represent the particular typeface selected. Final output varies based on the type and quality of the printer, and the fineness of the image, but it is possible to achieve results that rival those of a commercial typesetter.

Traditionally type is available as a single font, that is, one typeface in one style and one size, for example Bodoni (typeface) bold (style) 12 point (size); or as a scalable font, one that is programmed to be set in a wide range of sizes that are selected by the user. In either case, the type is assigned two files, one to create the characters for printing and another, called the screen font, to create the character for viewing on a monitor screen. Most of these fonts are programmed to be proportionately spaced, that is, they occupy the space required by the size of the letter with just enough white space between letters to balance out the words and make the text more readable. By contrast, fixed spacing such as found on a typewriter requires that each letter occupy the same amount of space.

Tip: Professional typographers deal in points and picas, and most computer programs have followed that lead. There are 72 points to an inch, which means that 1/16 inch equals 4½ points. A pica is 12 points, or 6 to the inch, slightly less than 3/16 of an inch. Many programs offer the user a selection of the system of measure, such as points, inches (and tenths of an inch), or metric, but it's a good idea to get used to type and line spacing in terms of points.

Scalable fonts have swept the market as they tend to be inexpensive and convenient, allowing the purchase of one font in one style as opposed to buying and loading a font for each size or a limited range of sizes.

Tip: Note that all scalable font packages are not created equal. Some of the packages that offer a large number of faces at giveaway prices include only a single style such as regular or roman for the face so that you can only view and print an emulation if you want bold or italics. The character set may also be scaled down so that special characters and accented characters are not available. Such a package may be adequate for display or headline type, but severely limiting for use as text.

A program that uses typographic fonts will almost assuredly permit precise line spacing, called leading. The programs may have a default leading that is approximately 120% of the type size; thus 10 point type is set on a 12 point line, 12 point on about a 14 point line, etc., and most allow the user to select the leading so that 10 point type can be set on an 11 point or 14 point line to suit a special purpose. Type set on a line that is less than 120% of the type size is said to be 'set tight'.

Tip: The point size of a type refers to the distance between the highest ascender and the lowest descender in the characters that make up the font. For that reason, point size is only a general reference to readability; a designer typeface with long ascenders and descenders and a small body size may appear much smaller than a more regularly proportioned face of the same point size.

Even a low–end GUI program should provide for precise sizing and spacing of type as well as the basic formatting features described above for non–graphics programs. That is where most of the similarities end.

Some special features are to be found in almost any word processing program; a larger number are offered on high–end programs:

- Standard layouts that can be attached to document files and that are programmed with such things as page size, margins, header, footer, paragraph styles, etc.

- Master layout pages within a document or extremely flexible header and footer sections that allow the user to set up headlines, borders, folios, graphics, or other material that repeats on every page;

- Formatted paragraph styles that permit the user to specify such things as typeface, font size, font style, type alignment, paragraph indent, line spacing, or tabs, and to mark paragraphs throughout a document with a particular style;

- The ability to create an index or table of contents from tagged items within a file;

- The linking of a series of document files to form a complete work, such as for the chapters of a book, and to index and paginate them as a unit;

- Annotation fields that allow notes or comments to be added to a document without changing the content of the document;

- Cross–referencing of subjects or captions in a document or series of documents;

- The precise or relative placement of graphics, that is, the ability to either specify an exact location for a graphic element on a page or to attach it to a block of copy so that if the block is moved, the graphic element moves with it;

- Automatic formatting of drop caps;

- Intuitive formatting of paragraphs with bullets or numbers;

- The capability of creating or importing a simple database or spreadsheet file;

- A merge feature that provides for linking a document file to a local or imported database for the purpose of creating a personalized mass mailing or placing a block of information in the file.

- The linking of other applications or utilities, such as a drawing program, a large dictionary, or a reference encyclopedia, so as to permit accessing them from inside the word processing program.

- The creation of macros to automate repetitive tasks.

Database Programs

A database is a collection of information contained in *records* that are made up of *fields* that each contain a specific item of information.

A simple database of names and addresses may look something like this on a monitor screen:

LASTNAME: Jones		FIRSTNAME: Jill	
ADDRESS: 17 Oak Street			
CITY: Anytown	STATE: Anystate		ZIP: 00000

All of this information taken together comprises a single database *record*. Each item of information such as LASTNAME is a *field*, and the titles in bold capital letters are *field names*.

Most programs permit the user considerable latitude in displaying a data entry form on the screen—some are quite sophisticated. In every case, the field name is protected, allowing the user to only enter data.

Fields are generally defined by type: a *character field* for text; a *number field* for numerical data that can be used in calculations; a *logic field* for providing one of two choices such as true or false, yes or no, or male or female; a *date field;* etc.

Field types are important in the validation, selection, and sorting of data. Validation is the technique for verifying the accuracy of data that is entered. For example, rejection of a number field entry that contains a letter will prevent errors in any future calculations or sorts based on that field; validation of a date field would reject an entry of 2/31/97; and a logic field can contain only one of two possible choices such as T/F, Y/N, or M/F.

Most fields are of a fixed length, that is, space is provided in memory for a finite number of characters that can be entered in the field. Customarily, the user sets the length of the field, based on anticipated need, although there are exceptions—a logic field allows for the entry of only one character; a date field size is normally set by the program based on the option selected for displaying dates.

A database can be relatively simple, as in the diagram above, or it can be extremely complex. There are two main characteristics that contribute to the complexity of a database and the difficulty one is likely to have in learning it: whether it is a flat file or relational, and whether or not it is programmable.

Flat File and Relational Databases

A flat file database is one in which all of the records are contained in a single computer file regardless of how many records there are or how many fields are contained in a record. A relational database program is one in which several files containing different information can be linked.

Relational databases are useful for such things as accounting programs in which different types of information, such as for accounts receivable, accounts payable, inventory, or payroll, are entered at different times and often different locations within a company, but that must be brought together from time to time to be summarized for various purposes.

An example of the way in which a relation database works is in the ordering and invoicing of merchandise sold by a company:

- When an order is entered, the operator enters the customer information—depending on the program, this may require typing a customer number, the first few letters of the customer's name, or selecting from a lookup table.

- The typing or selection prompts the computer to search the *Customer Database* for that specific customer and to enter on the order the name and address for that customer as well as any other pertinent information requested by the invoicing program such as a phone number, terms of the sale, method of shipping, etc.

- The items sold are each similarly typed or selected along with a quantity: the computer looks up the items in an *Inventory Database* and confirms that the merchandise is on hand, then enters a description of the items ordered .

- Once the items and quantity have been confirmed, the computer consults a *Cost/Price Database,* prices each item, and the *Order/Invoice Program* can calculate the complete cost for the merchandise plus any additional charges or discounts, and the order/invoice can be printed.

- Depending on the system employed by the company, a copy of the order with prices blanked out may go to a warehouse where the merchandise is selected and packed for shipping, and a copy of the invoice is sent to the customer.

- Downloading the invoice to an accounting program prompts the computer to adjust the *Inventory Database* quantity and update the *Accounts Receivable* database.

Thus, with four separate databases, *Customers, Inventory, Pricing,* and *Receivables,* working together in the *Order/Invoice Program* we have placed an order, shipped it, adjusted inventory and updated the customer's account. The beauty of all this is that it required only a single document with most of the typing automated.

Why four separate databases? Because a single, flat database would require repetitive entry of all our inventory and pricing information on each customer record in the database.

- The *Customer Database* requires that we enter information about the customer only once and, if it is carefully checked for accuracy, no matter how many orders the customer places, the information will always be accurate. In addition, the account information insures that when such things as terms or discounts change, we don't have to send out a memo to everyone in the office; the information pops up when an order is entered.

- The *Inventory Database*, if properly maintained with quantities posted when new merchandise is received, keeps us informed at all times of the quantity on hand or of the introduction of new merchandise. We can also set minimum quantities, so that when the inventory level is below a certain point, we are reminded to reorder.

- The *Cost/Price Database* (sometimes a part of the *Inventory Database*) also permits entry of a price in only one place with the assurance that whenever a price is changed it will be reflected in all subsequent orders.

• Programming the computer to post *Accounts Receivable* directly from the invoice assures that the client's account will reflect exactly the amount shown on the invoice sent to him and her.

To sum up, we've combined several clerical tasks and reduced our workload while minimizing the opportunity for error.

And how does the computer know what to do next? We've embedded commands and links to a common field in the *Customer Number* or *Name* and *Merchandise Number* or *Description* fields of the order entry form so that when the computer detects the presence of the cursor, a hot key combination, or typing in those fields it makes the appropriate response using the designated lookup table.

Similarly, whenever a quantity is entered, the program links the entry form to the *Cost/Price Database* through the common *Merchandise Number* or *Merchandise Description* field, checks for an out–of–stock condition, and if it does not detect one, inserts a price. Formulas in the data entry form then calculate the total cost.

Programmable Databases

A programmable database is by far the most flexible, allowing the creation of complex applications, but they are not designed for casual users as they require at least some familiarity with programming language.

One who is not a programmer can create surprisingly elaborate programs with a relational database that provides commands and options selected from a menu. Most programs guide the user·through the steps to creating useful applications and some even provide a programming language for advanced users.

Spreadsheets

A computer spreadsheet looks somewhat like an accountant's handwritten worksheet, with data arranged in rows and columns. The difference, however, is not only the automation of tasks, but flexibility that permits a range of uses that the poor accountant would never have predicted in his or her wildest dreams.

A Simple Spreadsheet

First, let's look at the basics. A spreadsheet might be used in a household or business to set up a budget, compare expenses, or to track investments. Any of these examples would require a list of specific items, one on each line or row, down the left–hand column of the sheet. Across the top we might label the columns with the months of the year.

	A	B	C	D	E
1	Item	Budget	Jan	Feb	Mar
2	Rent				
3	Utilities				
4	Food				
5	Clothing				
6	Auto				
7	Savings				
8	Total				

To set up our budget, we first determine how much we plan to spend for each item and enter the amount in the appropriate cell. When we come to the bottom cell, the Total, we enter a simple formula that tells the computer to add all of the numbers listed above. The precise syntax for that formula will vary with the program, but it is indeed simple. Then we copy that formula across the Total row so that each month as we fill in the amount of expense, the sum of those amounts will appear in the cell at the bottom of the column.

Tip: Copying a spreadsheet formula is a bit different from copying text in a document in that the formula adjusts for the move. Thus a formula that is written to total the amounts between Column B Row 2 (Budget-Rent) and column B row 7 (Budget-Savings) when copied to Column C Row 8 (Jan-Total) will adjust to address the cells from Rent to Savings in the Jan column. Got that? Good.

We probably want totals for the year to date as well, so we'll extend our spreadsheet out to Dec and add an additional column for totals by item. Again, we'll enter a formula at the end of the Rent row that identifies the cells we want to include in the total (C2 to N2— you don't want to include column B 'cause that's the budget), then we'll copy the formula down the rest of the rows.

Most programs provide an even easier and more intuitive way to set up this kind of formula—*named ranges*. A named range is a group of contiguous cells that are assigned a specific and unique name. With this feature we can name the block of cells from B2 to B7 *budget*, C2 to C7 *Jan*, and so on. To total those cells (using the appropriate syntax, of course) we simply enter a formula that says "total *Budget*", "total *Jan*", etc. And we can do the same across the page, but wait...

Let's rethink this business of adding cells across the page. Supposing we want to know how we're doing as the year progresses. We could insert a column following the Feb column and each monthly column thereafter. We could then insert a command in the cells of the column following Feb that instruct the computer to total Jan and Feb, after Mar to add Mar to the total and so on.

But after all, we really want to know how well we're doing compared to our budget, so now that we're into this programming thing why not add to the two month, three month, etc. formula an instruction to subtract two months or three months of budgeted rent, utilities, food, etc. Thus if we subtract our budget for actual a negative number would show how much we saved, and a positive number the amount we went over budget.

This should give you some idea of what can be done with the simplest of spreadsheets. Once the sheet is set up, all you have to do is enter the numbers and let the computer do the calculations. And if over the course of the year you want to make changes, you can do so, adding columns, rows, and formulas as you see fit. When you want to track business expenses, create a sales report, or whatever, the principal is the same.

Tip: The spreadsheet we suggested above will run to 25 columns (Item, Budget, 12 months, and 11 year-to-date totals). If you don't want to pan past the end of the screen to see the entire year, consider two spreadsheets, one with only the budgeted and monthly expense, the other with the year–to–date totals. The formulas will be the same— you don't have to be next to the cells to add them up; you can reference cells from anywhere in a spreadsheet file.

Layered Spreadsheets

Some spreadsheet programs support multiple sheets or pages in a single spreadsheet file. This is particularly useful when large amounts of accumulated data need to be summarized. Business expenses by type or sales by territory, for example, can be recorded on a different sheet for each month, then summarized on another sheet that references the cells containing totals for each of the items on the monthly sheets. The advantage of connecting sheets in this fashion is that the summary sheet is automatically updated whenever a change is made to one of the monthly sheets.

The Spreadsheet as a Database

The spreadsheet is not limited to the manipulation of numbers. Although much more limited that a relational database program, a spreadsheet program can be employed to set up a database for a variety of uses.

You can, for example, list names, addresses, and telephone numbers down the columns of a spreadsheet. Most have a sort capability that permits the user to sort rows based on the entries in any of the columns so that entries can be sorted by last name, area code, zip code, etc.

We've run into a couple of situations where this capability for sorting came in handy:

- **Year-end inventory**—For a medium-sized business that had materials scattered throughout three buildings we recorded the inventory tickets on a spreadsheet as they came in. Sorting by name and then by part number enabled us to combine like items and correct erroneous descriptions. When it came time to spot check the inventory, we sorted by location and printed out a list for each.

- **Tracking employees**—The company hires a number of seasonal employees, part-timers, and casual labor. Marriages during the off season that changed the last name of female employees, errors in recording Social Security numbers, and employees who used a given name one year and a nickname the next often gave us problems. A spreadsheet listing allowed sorting by last name and then again by Social Security number to weed out the duplicates.

Granted, you can do all of this with a database, but if you don't have one, or if the task is a simple one, a spreadsheet may be the best solution.

Other Features

There are a number of other capabilities that can enhance the versatility and thus the usefulness of a spreadsheet program:

- The creation of sophisticated reports with the use of special typefaces, headlines, and graphics.

- The acceptance of embedded sound or video files.

- The exporting or importing of data to or from another spreadsheet program, a word processing program or a database.

- The linking of data that provides for updates of information to and from a linked cell contained in another spreadsheet or a document.

Integrated Software

For those who prefer separate or dedicated programs for word processing, database management, and a spreadsheet, but don't require all the bells and whistles of a high–end program, an application that contains all three, called integrated software, may provide a satisfactory and inexpensive solution.

The programs in an integrated package are generally the easiest to learn while providing sufficient flexibility for most home or office workstations. Some even include a communications package and provide sufficient power to perform some basic desktop publishing functions.

Paint & Draw Programs

Art programs generally provide a number of tools for drawing lines, geometric shapes, etc.; a pointing tool used to select and move objects; a mechanism for changing line weight; and various methods for adding, removing, or graduating color.

The graphics in a paint program are created as a raster or bitmapped image, one that is made up small dots called pixels, while a draw program creates a vector image, one typified by smoother lines.

Basic programs provide limited means for the creation and editing of most graphic images, are easy to learn, and adequate for producing simple logos, line drawings, or illustrations. More advanced programs that are designed to create more sophisticated artwork and to manipulate full color photographs are used to prepare such things as magazine covers and advertising illustrations. These upscale programs can fulfill the wildest dreams of almost any illustrator, but they do require a powerful computer, adequate time for learning the program, and, in spite of the advertiser's promises, a fair measure of artistic talent to turn out those wonderful pieces of art.

In a nutshell, most of get along fine with a minimal program even though we occasionally crave some of the more advanced features; however, if you have an aptitude for art and a yearning to try your hand at it, by all means consider a high end program.

Tip: Even high end programs vary in the options they offer, the way in which they manipulate graphics, and in ease of learning. If you intend to invest in an expensive program, find a vendor who will let you try out a couple. If you talk it up, you may run across users of different programs who can help you make a decision based on their comments and output.

Drafting and Design

Some of our best ideas spring to life on the back of a cocktail napkin, but if their potential is to be realized, sooner or later they wind up as scaled drawings. The computer programs intended for the creation of scaled drawings are many and varied, from general purpose applications to those designed for specific tasks:

• A general purpose program is likely to be more difficult to master than one devoted to creating a particular type of drawing, but that's partly because it is intended to satisfy almost any drafting or design requirement.

- In addition to tools similar to those found in a drawing program for sketching lines, circles, rectangles, etc. and a pointing tool used to select and move objects, a drafting program should provide a set of dimension templates. These are straight and curved lines with arrows on each end to used to indicate sizes, and creating them from scratch can be tedious.

- The program will likely offer sets of images that represent such things as doorways, windows, electrical devices, etc. as well as tools to ease the task of creating new ones.

- Most vendors offer, as well, sets of templates or images dedicated to a particular type of drawing such as for building construction, woodworking designs, interior design, electrical plans, etc. that can be added to the program.

Anyone in a business that requires a considerable amount of drawing or drafting such as an interior designer, a landscaper, toolmaker, electrician, cabinet or furniture maker, etc. should be able to find programs intended for that particular business.

Communications

Communications software permits the transfer of data between computers or computer systems. Faxing from the computer or accessing data from the web requires specific software designed to make the connections and authorize the transfer of data.

Special software is also required for sending and receiving E-mail or voice mail, or even communicating over a peer–to–peer network, a direct connection that links two or more computers.

Choice of software is largely dictated by the hardware and the type of system you are connecting to.

Special Applications

It's not terribly difficult to set up a database of names and addresses or of favorite recipes; or to track household expenses or investments with the aid of a spreadsheet. You could keep track of appointments with a word processor and even design a house with a paint or drawing program. But if you are not moved to 'setting up' things, or feel that you need some extra guidance, there are numerous programs available to ease specific tasks and that offer loads of gratuitous advice along the way.

The range of these special programs is far to great to list them all here, but we'll try to give you some idea of the sort of programs that are available:

Household Finance

A household finance package should contain a basic household budget with instructions and advice to guide you through setting one up for yourself. Many provide additional features as well:

- Recommendations for budgeted amounts based on information that is fed into the programs such as household income, number and ages of family members, and lifestyle.

- Advice for controlling expenditures.

- A register for recording payments, whether by check or cash.

- A simple, easy to follow system for reconciling your checking account with a statement from the bank.

- Some means to distinguish those expenditures that are business related or tax deductible.

- A means for recording and comparing actual expenses to the budgeted amounts.

- The ability to set college fund or retirement goals, with guidance on how to achieve them including some sophisticated calculations, such as for the future value of regular savings at a fixed rate of interest, or the amount that needs to be set aside to accumulate a given amount by a specified date.

A personal finance program may also have the ability to track stock and bond performance. The serious investor, however, will probably want to search out a package devoted to tracking investments, perhaps even one that can connect through a modem to call up stock prices and that permits the buying and selling of stock through an on-line service.

Business Finance

Business packages range from an accounting program simple enough to be used by someone with little or no experience in accounting to one that requires an accountant of some experience to set up and run.

Any financial management package should allow the user to set up accounts to suit his or her needs and to summarize the contents of those accounts in a balance sheet, income statement, cash flow statement, and a dated accounts payable or accounts receivable report.

The flexibility in setting up reports, however, will vary from one program to another; the user may be limited to reports that list every account, or there may be provision for collapsing subaccounts to produce condensed reports, for example.

There are a number of other features that may be contained in an accounting program:

- A provision for repetitive entries; that is, the scheduling of regular weekly or monthly payments for automatic entry on specific dates or at regular intervals.

- The ability to set due dates and discounts for payables and receivables for all accounts, by individual account, or by invoice.

- Pop–up reminders that appear when bills are due to be paid or when payments are due from clients.

- Automation of the payment process that enables the user to call up a list of bills that are due, to specify whether all are to be paid or only those individually selected, then to print out the checks and post the payments.

- To connect to the bank through an on–line service for up–to–the–minute information about one's bank account and to transfer funds between accounts or for the payment of bills.

- A payroll program that provides for:
  - the entry of information about each employee such as rate of pay and exemptions;
  - company pay policy such as for paid holidays and overtime rates;
  - the calculation of pay and deductions based on hours entered;
  - the printing of payroll checks; and
  - the calculation and preparation of paperwork such as for periodic payments to the IRS and W–2's for employees.

- A warning when the user attempts to make an improper entry, especially in a program designed for those inexperienced in accounting.

- An equipment record and amortization tables that calculate the amount to be allowed for periodic depreciation for each piece of equipment based on original cost, anticipated life, scrap value, etc.

Household Inventory

A program that assists in listing and valuing all of a family's household articles. And it's not just to see who has the most toys! Kept in a safe place, it can be an invaluable aid to filing an insurance claim after a fire or other disaster. It's also an excellent tool for making sure that the insurance you carry is ade-

quate—you may be surprised at the replacement cost
of your possessions

Sure, you can do this on a spreadsheet, but will you
remember all of the smaller items tucked away in a
drawer or hanging on the wall? or that grandma's an-
tique china should be appraised in order to be properly protected by insurance? A good program will offer
a variety of such tips and reminders. Besides, taking
inventory is a tedious job and any encouragement you
can get, even if it's from a computer program bent on
sticking its nose into your business, is bound to help.

Business Planning

So you want to start a business? or expand an existing one? There are packages for the budding entre-
preneur or the hardened veteran that can:

- Help lay out the costs for startup, assess manufacturing cost at various levels of production, and
  perhaps even recommend sources of information
  about markets for distribution.

- Assist in writing an organized business plan from
  the concept to startup costs to potential, and that
  can print out a set of professional looking documents that can be taken to potential investors or
  creditors.

- Recommend sources for financing and, in some cases, guide you through the process, such as the steps and paperwork required to apply for a Small Business Administration loan.

Most of us look at a business startup or expansion with stars in our eyes. A good planning package will serve to remind us of some of the things we may not have considered.

Business planning is also important in the management of an existing business or of an ongoing project. For that purpose there are a number of programs:

- Scheduling or timekeeping programs that aid in plotting equipment time or manning requirements for the completion of a project or series of projects.

- Project managers that allow the user to establish a date for completion of a complex project and help establish a time line that indicates when specific tasks related to the project must be completed.

- 'What if' programs that determine the burden placed on equipment, personnel, and cash flow at various levels of production, and that can help in judging the true cost of an expansion or cutback in production.

Tax Preparation

Regardless of how much we dislike paying our personal income tax, it pales beside our distaste for the paperwork involved. A tax package can help with the paperwork so that we can focus our resentment on the tax itself.

A tax package queries you for the same information that you would normally write in on the tax forms or forms, then fills out and prints the forms that you have to file with the IRS. Probably not of great interest to anyone who files a 1040EZ, but for those who have major deductions, receive investment income, are self-employed, or use part of their home for business, a tax program can simplify the task of finding and filling out all of those extra forms.

A good tax program should provide:

• Ease of entry—You don't fill out the forms or make any calculations, the program does. You simply fill out a questionnaire provided by the program based on information you give it regarding sources of income, type of employment, etc.

• Related information and reminders—The program should offer advice and counsel along the way such as for limitations on deductions, carrying a business loss forward or backward, or deferring income. Certain entries should trigger reminder lists of things you may have forgotten. Noting that you are self–employed or use part of your home for business purposes, for example, should bring up a list of possible deductions that you may have overlooked.

- All of the forms required to file your tax return.

- A means to update the program each year to incorporate changes in the tax rates and tax law.

Tip: Chances are, if your return is complicated, the program will miss something, especially if it involves a last minute change in the legislature. With a significant amount of money at stake, it is probably wise to have a professional review the forms; advance preparation of forms for the preparer should still save you time and money.

Travel

Traveling for pleasure can be enhanced by a program that provides information about a particular area such as places of interest, currency, and language. The best programs will include full color graphics and maps of the area.

Travel by auto with a portable computer can be enhanced with a map and locator program. A good up–to–date mapping program features wide area maps that permit focusing in on a street map of a city or to a view that takes in only a few city blocks. Some allow the user to select a destination, then guide him or her to the location. Especially remarkable are those that link to a satellite which can pinpoint the motorist's position, provide explicit instructions for travel to the selected site, and sound an alert when a wrong turn is taken or a turn is missed.

For those who travel extensively by air there are programs for accessing airline schedules, discount information, and that let you make, change, or cancel reservations through a service provider.

Address Book

One of the basic files set up by most of us when we first begin using a database, but a commercial application usually offers more options than the beginner is able or willing to take the time to program.

In addition to recording name, address, and telephone number, most programs provide for:

- Designation of entries as personal or business;

- The recording of important dates such as birthdays and anniversaries, often with a reminder that pops up a specified number of days prior to the event; and

- Space for recording special event cards or gifts that have been given or received.

Name and address packages designed especially for business use provide such things as space for notes about the client and his or her company, a record of each contact, and a reminder to set up an appointment for a future meeting either at a designated time or after a certain period.

Appointment Book

An appointment book is often coupled with an address book, but some are stand–alone programs that double as a planner. A good appointment book provides:

- A calendar page for each day that permits scheduling of appointments, meetings, etc. in 15 to 30 minute increments.

- A pop–up reminder that can be attached to any scheduled event and be preset for a specific time such as a day or an hour in advance of the appointment.

- Space for notes about topics to be discussed, preparation or materials required, etc.

- A separate task list for personal responsibilities as well as duties that have been assigned to others with pop–up notes that warn of impending deadlines.

Some business applications link a number of users through a local office network and coordinate their task lists, or plan meetings to fit the schedules of those involved.

Home Design Kit

Here's a program intended for those who want to lay out their dream house.

The program is likely to be short on tools for creating extremely sophisticated customized drawings, but it should provide:

- A number of sample layouts or floor plans;

- A variety of templates for such things as doors and windows, and the ability to alter their size and placement;

- Patterns for indicating different types of materials such as wood, concrete, stone, or brick that can be used to fill in portions of a templates to indicate their construction.

- The ability to create both a floor plan or top view, and side views.

More sophisticated programs offer a rotating tool that permits viewing a representation of the house design from any angle in either a transparent drawing that shows the relative position of every part of the house or a landscape view that shows the outside of the house complete with trees and shrubbery.

Probably none of these programs will give you a complete list of materials, fulfill all of your local building code requirements, or furnish blueprints you can take to a builder, but they will most certainly make your designer's job easier and less expensive as well as assuring that the final product will more nearly resemble what you envisioned.

Interior Design

An interior design application for home or office permits the user to set up a schematic of a room including the positions of doors, windows, and other permanent objects, then allows placement of furniture or equipment. Such a program should provide:

- Stock templates for various pieces of furniture or office machines;

- The ability to produce custom templates by altering those furnished or creating new ones;

- Advice for providing 'clear space' or a work area around objects when necessary;

This is certainly not a program we need every day, but it's easier to learn than a general use drafting pro-

gram, and when you think about the alternative—
moving all that furniture around several times before
deciding what works...

Recipes & Cooking

You can even cook with the computer! Well, not exactly, but you can get a host of new recipes and record your favorites from other sources in any one of a
number of recipe programs.

Like the cookbooks you are probably already accustomed to, the quality of the recipes and the clarity of
instructions vary from one to another. Personally,
we're attracted to computer recipe programs for other
reasons:

• The ability to catalogue our favorite recipes. The
  program should provide a simple method for
  adding recipes to those furnished.

• The ability to adapt recipes for quantity. When we
  need less or more than a particular recipe provides, we don't want to do the math. Some programs base all recipes on the number of servings,
  then adapt the ingredients list to the number of
  servings you specify.

• The option of calling up a list of recipes by type,
  such as appetizer, soup, or meat course, or by
  the main ingredient. You should be able to clas-

sify the recipes you add by type or the main ingredients that you specify.

- Instructions and warnings about substitutions in a recipe.

- Preparation of a shopping list. The cook selects the recipes and number of servings, say, for a dinner party. The computer then combines the ingredients in a single list that we can pare down to those ingredients that we don't have on hand.

- Sidebars or help notes that offer advice in selecting ingredients, careful guidance through an uncommon technique, and tips that can make preparation easier.

- A guest log where we can record the dates when we entertained, who was present, and what was served.

- Information about sources for exotic foods and cookware.

There are a considerable number of cooking and recipe programs designed for the neophyte as well as for the experienced cook.

Learning Programs

Computers have been used in classrooms for ages; just ask your kids. They are used regularly in business as well, to teach new employees about a company, its products, and policies; and to train employees in the operation of new or unfamiliar equipment and techniques.

Videos are often used for training, both in school and in business, but for a teaching aid that allows a person to progress at his or her own rate and to stop at any point and pick up later at the same place, you can't beat a computer.

Now you can bring learning into the home with programs that teach typing, a language, music and art appreciation, or a host of high school and college courses. There are even programs that teach us how to use other programs. Wonder if there are any for learning about learning courses...?

Utilities

A *utility* is a software package that can enhance the operation of the computer or of a specific program, or to assist the user by improving productivity. A utility may be designed to:

- Speed computer processing or printing
- Manage memory
- Provide screen savers or other graphics
- Perform system backups at regular intervals

- Provide a calculator or calendar

- Furnish a timer or pop-up reminders

- Scan for viruses

- Compress files

- Manage graphics

- Delete applications or unnecessary files

System Performance

Despite vendors' claims, there doesn't seem to be any hard evidence that a software program can measurably increase the speed of processing. There may be some merit in the claims of those utilities that profess to speed printing or improve the quality of output, although with printer manufacturers eyeing the same goal as the software developer, it's very likely that any newer printers are going to incorporate enhancements similar to those offered in a software package.

Memory Manager

Memory managers toil to squeeze the most out of a computer. They provide for the conservation of RAM in order to provide maximum space for loading programs. They also convert extended and expanded memory. A decade ago it was common for a computer to come equipped with 520K (kilobytes) of memory

(RAM), or 640K, the most memory that DOS would recognize. An early technique for providing additional working space for programs was the installation of expanded memory and a memory manager that worked around the DOS limitation so that the added memory could be used by programs written to take advantage of it. Newer technology uses extended memory to do roughly the same thing, but much faster. Unfortunately some programs only recognize expanded memory, so that a memory manager is required not only to convince DOS to use the memory over 640K, but also to sense whether extended or expanded memory is required and to convert that extra RAM to the proper type of memory.

Windows, of course, creates a graphic environment as well as supplying memory management. There are lesser known utilities that provide a graphic environment as well, and some that enhance Windows' interface. One of them marks your place at the time you shut down the computer, so that when you reboot, it takes you back to the place where you were working immediately before the shutdown.

Screen Savers

Screen savers have become a very popular and sometimes amusing addition to today's PC. Back in the stone age (a couple of decades ago), computer monitor screens that were left on for long periods of time with the same pattern on the screen eventually wound up with a ghost of that pattern burned into the screen. Remember the ping–pong game we used to play on the television screen that eventually burned an image of the court on that screen? We may have been stuck with that image on the television, but the prospect of a similar image on a computer screen opened a lucrative market for a host of utilities that blanked the screen or created a variety of fascinating images after a short period of inactivity.

These days that problem has been largely eliminated. New technology has aided in the creation of screens that are not so susceptible to having an image burned into them. Moreover, power conservation techniques incorporated into most newer computers provide for shutting down the screen after a designated period of inactivity. Enhanced graphics and the creativity of developers have maintained the popularity of screen savers, nonetheless. The bottom line is that you probably don't need a screen saver—but you will probably get one because they are fun.

Backup Systems

If your work at any given time is concentrated in a limited number of files, you may be satisfied with backing up those few files at the end of a work day.

On the other hand, if your activities encompass a broad range of programs and files, or if you never seem to get around to backing up your work, an automatic backup system may be just what you need. Just as we advise saving work often to minimize the loss of data when the power goes down, we strongly urge regular backups to minimize loss if the computer goes down. You only need to lose an important chunk of data one time to become a believer.

A backup system may be as simple as a reminder that pops up on the screen at regular intervals, say every Friday afternoon, or it may be a fully automated tape or disk drive that is programmed to go into action when you're not around, in the middle of the night, for example. A quality software package should have the capacity to be programmed for a full backup, that is, to copy everything on the computer, or for an update that copies only those files that have changed since the last backup.

Popup Reminders

Those popup reminders aren't limited to backup programs—they are an excellent way to draw your attention to an appointment or prompt you to return a call. If you are working at home, they may also remind you that it's someone else's turn to use the computer!

Tip: A word about TSR's: TSR stands for Terminate and Stay Resident, and is descriptive of those programs or utilities that are loaded into areas of the same precious memory used to operate all programs. Even when inactivated or terminated, a TSR remains in memory ready to be called up in a fraction of a second. Some are system drivers over which the user has little or no control; others such as screen savers or pop-up memos are activated by the user. The point is that we sometimes need to be careful about loading too many trivial devices and not allowing sufficient room for more important programs to function.

Controlling Viruses

A computer virus is a generally undesirable and unwanted program file or routine that can corrupt files, replicate itself, replicate other files, or in some other way degrade a computer system and perhaps shut it down. There are a number of packages available on the market to detect and eliminate a virus, including some provided as supplements to other programs such as operating systems.

It's well worth the short time it takes to run a virus program from time to time, especially before installing files from a disk or when downloading from a remote source.

Tip: Most of us think we're safe when we don't surf the net or load illegal software, but viruses have found their way into new software—apparently in products that were returned and repackaged. Most reputable vendors do not repackage software, but why take a chance?

New viruses spring up from time to time as certain hackers strive to prove how smart they are, so it's a good idea to regularly upgrade an antivirus program. No need to be overly alarmed about contracting a virus, because most of us haven't, but there's no harm in playing safe either.

File Compression

Compression utilities employ a number of techniques for reducing the amount of space a computer file requires on a storage medium. Their purpose, of course, is to allow for the storage of more data in less space.

There are stand–alone utilities available as well some provided as add–ons with other programs, such as an operating system, a graphics file management program, or a disk cleanup program (see below). Some are designed to compress only specific files or directories selected by the user, others compress the entire contents of a hard drive.

These compression utilities vary from one another in their purpose and function:

• One may require that a file or files be selected

and restored from within the utility program before they can be used, or it may restore automatically when a file is selected or called up from within a program.

- The time it takes for a file to be restored may be discernible, or the user may not notice any significant delay in bringing the up files.

When selecting a compression utility, consider:

- Whether you really need one—opening unnecessary space on a hard drive is a poor trade-off for slower performance;

- How convenient it is to restore files with a particular program; and

- How often you expect to use the files being compressed—compression is not a bad way to archive old data files or even seldom-used programs, but if restoration noticeably slows access, you certainly don't want to use it for programs you operate regularly.

Whether or not you install your own file compression utility, you will likely use one. Most program and graphics files these days are compressed when you buy them, then decompressed when you install them in your computer.

Graphic Image Management

Chances are that over time you will accumulate a host of graphic image files. Even if you don't answer any of the ads or mailings that promise thousands of images on a CD, the ones that come gratuitously with the programs you install will begin to pile up. In fact, very few programs are sold today without the promise of 'hundreds of clip art images and fonts'. Ironically, if you purchase a graphic image management program, you'll probably get another few hundred images with it as well, but you will also get the means to keep track of everything.

As with any type of program, features vary, but a good program should provide for:

• Importation of a wide variety of image formats. That means at least 20 of the most common formats, especially those recognized by the desktop publishing, word processing, etc. programs that you use regularly.

• Conversion and exportation of images in a similarly wide variety of formats, and the ability to convert the exported image to a different graphic format.

• The organizing of imported images into user-designated groups or libraries.

• The viewing on screen of groups of thumbnail

copies of the images in a particular library with the ability to view each at full size as well.

- The option of storing image files uncompressed, or for compression of the files to save disk space.

You may also want:

- To be able to print out thumbnail reference sheets for a particular library or a set of images that features a number of representations on a single page with descriptive data for each including such things as file name, format, and original size.

- The capability of compressing and storing document files, providing a convenient system for archiving older or inactive files that you may need again someday.

- Features that allow the manipulation of a graphics file such as resizing, inverting, or rotating an image before saving or exporting it.

Keep in mind that this type of utility generally saves the images in database groups or library files so that using an image requires calling up the program, selecting the image desired, and exporting it. Most will consider this a small inconvenience, however, compared to that of being able to catalog and then easily sift through a large number of graphic images.

Disk Cleanup

For most of us, the days are gone when a program occupied a single directory that could be deleted or archived on a floppy disk when it was no longer needed. Simply deleting a program's directory in most of today's systems leaves behind a host of configuration files and links to the operating system or operating environment.

Any of several programs designed to uninstall other programs automate the task as well as providing solutions to some other problems. An uninstall program should be equipped to:

- Monitor the installation of new applications, utilities, etc. and keep a record of them so as to provide a complete cleanup of unnecessary files if the program is removed.

- Provide an analysis of an application slated for deletion including a list of files outside the program's directory that are recommended for removal, cautioning against removal of files that may be shared with another program, and allowing the user to approve deletion of specific files.

- Remove a program and its directory from a hard drive including any linking or configuration files that the original installation placed in other directories, subject to approval of the user.

- Remove any references to a deleted program contained in a configuration file of the operating system or another program.

- Locate orphan files; that is, configuration or data files that are not linked to any of the programs currently on the computer.

- Create a compressed backup file of all deletions so that they can be restored if necessary.

A program that deletes programs should be able to archive them as well. An archived program is simply compressed with all of its links intact. The couple of minutes it takes to restore a seldom–used archived program is a small price to pay for regaining a few megabytes of precious disk space.

Security

One only has to read a few of the stories that crop up from time to time about hackers getting into government or corporate computer files to realize that no data is truly safe. But there are programs that offer a modicum of security, and that's all most of us need— just enough to keep a casual surfer from stumbling across sensitive company data or to lock the kids out of our Christmas list.

Keyboard lockout, controlled by the turn of a key in a

lock on the computer console, shuts off communication between the computer and the keyboard, effectively shutting out anyone from using the computer.

Password protection that requires entry of a string of characters or symbols when the computer boots up can similarly shut out anyone who does not know the password.

But supposing we share a computer with someone else at home or in the office or share computer programs across a network. Other levels of security are possible with most programs:

- Password protection that limits the use of a program to authorized personnel.

- Within a program, individual documents and files can often be protected by a password—a good way to share programs with the kids while preventing them from rewriting the company newsletter or playing hob with its financial statements.

Some programs, such as integrated accounting software, may provide a number of levels of protection—different passwords limit access to certain files or functions as set by the user or users with a password at the highest level.

Managing Your Computer

Once the hardware is set up and all of the software is installed, it's time to...

Okay, make sure everything works,

try a few games,

get familiar with the apps,

...there. Had enough? Then it's time to get organized!

Just a few notes about things we tend to put off until we get into trouble.

Documentation

Make sure that the serial numbers for the computer, printer, and any other hardware or software are recorded on the receipts, then file them in a safe place. Most equipment will have a plate on the back with the serial number on it. Serial numbers for software may be on the installation disk or on documentation that comes with them. Check the user's manual that came with the item if you have any trouble finding a serial number. You will need the number in order to register the hardware or software with the manufacturer.

Most user's manuals include a help line telephone number—you may want to record a serial number there as well, because you will need it if you have to call for assistance. Considering all of the hardware and software we've purchased over the last few years, we've had precious little need for a help line, but it's comforting to know that it's there.

You'll probably want to keep the user's manuals close at hand for a time, then be sure to file them in a safe place as well. We've often found that after months of using an application, we needed to go back to the manuals for information about a feature that we hadn't had occasion to use before.

Software Backups

Most software vendors recommend making a backup copy of installation disks before attempting to install the program and it's good advice to heed. In fact we assure that our backup disks are good by using them for the initial installation. Keep the extra disks in a secure place such as a safe deposit box, especially if you have a lot of high end apps that would be expensive to replace.

Organizing Directories and Files

Applications ordinarily save data files to a default directory; most allow the user to change that default. We usually can't find a reason to change the default directory for specialty apps such as an accounting program, a tax program, or home inventory. Files from a general purpose application such as a word processor or spreadsheet, however, can be many and varied.

Frankly, we find scrolling through a hundred or more files trying to guess what's in them to be a real pain, so we've organized our files in directories separate from the apps in which they were created. In fact, most directories contain files from more than one application:

- A number of directories named for our clients may include copies of correspondence or documentation associated with a project created in a word processing program as well as reports for the client produced with a spreadsheet program.

- The PROJECT directory contains ideas, research, anticipated cost, and perhaps prospects for projects that we think have some merit, but that have not been sold.

- The PROPOSAL directory contains information about presentations made to clients and prospects. Isolating this material from the client directories permits us to easily draw on completed presentations when we're preparing a new one.

• The COMPANY directory contains a database of clients and prospects, a database of information sources, a spreadsheet for travel expenses, etc.

Others who share a computer may find it more convenient to set up a directory for each user with subdirectories that more specifically define their output. Organize your work in directories that best suit your work habits and style, but we strongly urge that you set them up for maximum productivity.

Backing Up Data

Because reconstructing data can be a painful (and sometimes hopeless) process, we've choose to end this section with an important bit of advice:

Back up your work often and keep a copy in a secure place

Notes

Notes